Follies

Kurt Peterson as YOUNG BEN, Virginia Sandifur as
YOUNG PHYLLIS, Alexis Smith as PHYLLIS and
John McMartin as BEN.

FOLLIES
A Musical

BOOK BY
James Goldman

MUSIC AND LYRICS BY
Stephen Sondheim

RANDOM HOUSE   NEW YORK

This book is meant for Julia
and it comes to her with love.

FOLLIES *was first presented on April 4, 1971, by Harold Prince, in association with Ruth Mitchell, at the Winter Garden Theatre in New York City, with the following cast:*

(In order of appearance)

MAJOR-DOMO	Dick Latessa
SALLY DURANT PLUMMER	Dorothy Collins
YOUNG SALLY	Marti Rolph
CHRISTINE DONOVAN	Ethel Barrymore Colt
WILLY WHEELER	Fred Kelly
STELLA DEEMS	Mary McCarty
MAX DEEMS	John J. Martin
HEIDI SCHILLER	Justine Johnston
CHAUFFEUR	John Grigas
MEREDITH LANE	Sheila Smith
ROSCOE	Michael Bartlett
DEEDEE WEST	Helon Blount
HATTIE WALKER	Ethel Shutta
EMILY WHITMAN	Marcie Stringer
THEODORE WHITMAN	Charles Welch
VINCENT	Victor Griffin
VANESSA	Jayne Turner
YOUNG VINCENT	Michael Misita
YOUNG VANESSA	Graciela Daniele
SOLANGE LA FITTE	Fifi D'Orsay
CARLOTTA CAMPION	Yvonne De Carlo
PHYLLIS ROGERS STONE	Alexis Smith
BENJAMIN STONE	John McMartin

YOUNG PHYLLIS	Virginia Sandifur
YOUNG BEN	Kurt Peterson
BUDDY PLUMMER	Gene Nelson
YOUNG BUDDY	Harvey Evans
DIMITRI WEISMANN	Arnold Moss
KEVIN	Ralph Nelson
YOUNG STELLA	Julie Pars
YOUNG HEIDI	Victoria Mallory
PARTY MUSICIANS:	Taft Jordan, Aaron Bell, Charles Spies, Robert Curtis.
SHOWGIRLS:	Suzanne Briggs, Trudy Carson, Kathie Dalton, Ursula Maschmeyer, Linda Perkins, Margot Travers.
SINGERS, DANCERS:	Graciela Daniele, Mary Jane Houdina, Sonja Lekova, Rita O'Connor, Julie Pars, Suzanne Rogers, Roy Barry, Steve Boockvor, Michael Misita, Joseph Nelson, Ralph Nelson, Ken Urmston, Peter Walker, Donald Weissmuller.

The SINGERS and DANCERS appear as GUESTS, WAITERS, WAITRESSES, PHOTOGRAPHERS, CHORUS GIRLS, CHORUS BOYS, etc.

Book by James Goldman
Music and lyrics by Stephen Sondheim
Choreography by Michael Bennett
Scenic production designed by Boris Aronson
Costumes by Florence Klotz
Lighting by Tharon Musser

Musical direction by Harold Hastings
Orchestrations by Jonathan Tunick
Dance music arrangements by John Berkman
Production directed by Harold Prince and Michael Bennett

MUSICAL NUMBERS

"Beautiful Girls"	ROSCOE AND COMPANY
"Don't Look at Me"	SALLY AND BEN
"Waiting for the Girls Upstairs"	BUDDY, BEN, PHYLLIS, SALLY, YOUNG BUDDY, YOUNG BEN, YOUNG PHYLLIS AND YOUNG SALLY
"Listen to the Rain on the Roof"	THE WHITMANS
"Ah, Paris!"	SOLANGE
"Broadway Baby"	HATTIE
"The Road You Didn't Take"	BEN
"Bolero d'Amour"	Danced by VINCENT and VANESSA
"In Buddy's Eyes"	SALLY
"Who's That Woman?"	STELLA AND COMPANY
"I'm Still Here"	CARLOTTA
"Too Many Mornings"	BEN AND SALLY
"The Right Girl"	BUDDY
"One More Kiss"	HEIDI AND YOUNG HEIDI
"Could I Leave You?"	PHYLLIS

✳✳

✳✳✳✳ *LOVELAND* ✳✳✳✳

THE FOLLY OF LOVE

"Loveland"	*Sung by The Ensemble*
The Spirit of First Love	*Miss Kathie Dalton*
The Spirit of Young Love	*Miss Margot Travers*

The Spirit of True Love	*Miss Suzanne Briggs*
The Spirit of Pure Love	*Miss Trudy Carson*
The Spirit of Romantic Love	*Miss Linda Perkins*
The Spirit of Eternal Love	*Miss Ursula Maschmeyer*

THE FOLLY OF YOUTH

Scene—A Bower in Loveland
  "You're Gonna Love Tomorrow"   *Sung by Mr. Ben Stone
and Miss Phyllis Rogers*
  "Love Will See Us Through"   *Sung by Mr. Buddy Plummer
and Miss Sally Durant*

BUDDY'S FOLLY

Scene—A Thoroughfare in Loveland
  "The God-Why-Don't-You-Love-Me Blues"   *Sung and
Danced by Mr. Buddy Plummer*
*(With the Assistance of Miss Suzanne Rogers and Miss Rita
O'Connor)*

SALLY'S FOLLY

Scene—A Boudoir in Loveland
  "Losing My Mind"   *Sung by Mrs. Sally Durant Plummer*

PHYLLIS'S FOLLY

Scene—A Honky-Tonk in Loveland
  "The Story of Lucy and Jessie"   *Sung by
Mrs. Phyllis Rogers Stone*
(Danced by Mrs. Stone and The Dancing Ensemble)

BEN'S FOLLY

Scene—A Supper Club in Loveland
  "Live, Laugh, Love"   *Sung by Mr. Benjamin Stone*
(Danced by Mr. Stone and The Dancing Ensemble)

✳✳✳

THE SCENE

A party on the stage of the Weismann Theater

THE TIME

Tonight

Follies

We see an old asbestos fire-curtain, caked with dust, unused for years. We hear soft tympani, like thunder from a long time ago. Slowly, the curtain starts to rise.

At first, we're not sure what we see. The stage is dim, gray and enormous. Then, as lights flash here and there, we see the shell, the remnants, all that's left of what was once a famous theater.

The stage itself is vast. The brick wall at the back is only partly there, vast chunks of the proscenium are missing. Along the sides are platforms made of metal scaffolding with floors of wooden planks. Beyond the back and sides is darkness, and we feel as if the theater stretched on forever.

Alone and motionless onstage, we see a SHOWGIRL. *She is tall and slim and beautiful. Her skin is unnaturally pale, her dress is black and white and clinging, simple yet extravagant.*

Music begins; soft, slow, romantic, strange. The SHOWGIRL *comes to life, as if she were a ghost who had been waiting in the theater for years for us to come. She moves as showgirls did— but slowly, almost drifting. From the darkness, out of nowhere, comes another* SHOWGIRL, *like the first, in black and white.*

Then, moving briskly through the ghosts, a MAJOR-DOMO *strides onstage, followed by a line of uniformed* WAITERS *and* WAITRESSES *carrying trays of glasses and other party equipment.*

They pass by the ghosts, not seeing them, and move offstage as, from the darkness, a group of six CHORUS GIRLS *comes into view. Young and lovely, dressed like the ghosts in black and white, they are singing and dancing something jazzy, but moving in slow motion, mouths opening and closing soundlessly.*

More WAITERS *and* WAITRESSES *cross busily; more ghosts appear. Four musicians, carrying their instruments, move briskly*

3

on, and climb a flight of stairs to a scaffolding platform where an upright piano and chairs stand waiting for them.

Far from us, in the midst of this, SALLY DURANT PLUMMER *comes running breathlessly onstage. She is blonde, petite, pert, sweet-faced and, at forty-nine, still remarkably like the girl she was thirty years ago.*

Flushed, terribly excited to be there, she looks around.

SALLY Oh Lord, don't tell me I'm the first.

MAJOR-DOMO *(Turning to her with a smile of welcome)* Good evening.

    (He politely reaches for the party invitation she is clutching in her hand. She gives it to him)

SALLY I couldn't wait, I guess. I haven't seen New York in thirty years and all my friends; I'm so excited. *(Moving downstage, taking in the theater)* What a shame. Why do they have to tear it down? *(As she moves, one of the six* CHORUS GIRLS *breaks from formation and goes slowly to* SALLY, *eyes riveted on her. It is* YOUNG SALLY, *the self, the girl that* SALLY *was in 1940.* SALLY, *not seeing her, turns smilingly to a* WAITRESS *who carries a mass of silk sashes over one arm)* You can't imagine how glamorous it was or what it meant to be a Weismann girl. The way it felt to come onstage, all those eyes looking at you . . . I'm Sally Durant Plummer. *(As the* WAITRESS *selects a sash and hands it to her)* I'm not going to recognize a soul. How pretty. Can I keep it? *(The* WAITRESS *nods and smiles and moves offstage. Speaking to her as she goes)* It's going to be a lovely party. I'm so glad I came.

    (The music rises. SALLY *moves to the wings while* YOUNG SALLY, *longing to follow her, is caught up by the* CHORUS GIRLS *as they dance past.*

And suddenly, the slow, strange music swells, strikes an expectant chord, and cuts to bright, light-hearted pastiche tunes of the twenties and thirties as . . .

The guests arrive. The stage is suddenly filled with color and energy, as couple after couple, ranging in age from their fifties to their eighties, move about excitedly. They make their way downstage, past ghostly SHOW-GIRLS, *to the* WAITRESS *with the sashes. She presents a sash to each lady, who moves with it to the wings as husbands and escorts mill about.*

In the midst of the excitement, BEN *and* PHYLLIS ROGERS STONE *arrive.* PHYLLIS *is a tall and queenly woman, stylish and intelligent. Her fine-boned face is probably more beautiful now than it was thirty years ago. Her husband* BEN *is tall, trim, distinguished; a successful and authoritative man. You feel as if you've seen them in* Vogue *and you probably have.*

As they move downstage, wryly taking in the scene, YOUNG PHYLLIS *detaches herself, just as* YOUNG SALLY *did, from the group of memory* CHORUS GIRLS *and moves to* PHYLLIS, *as if fascinated to see what she has become.*

And at the same time, from the shadows, YOUNG BEN *appears. Face pale, dressed all in gray, he moves to* BEN *and watches)*

PHYLLIS   Lord, will you look at it.

BEN   Another theater comes down.

PHYLLIS   It's progress; what this city needs is one more parking lot.

BEN   I like it: it's the way nostalgia ought to look. I sometimes wonder why our memories don't go the way these walls have gone. Our bodies do: our plaster flakes away

5

and yet the fool things we remember stay as fresh as paint. I can remember you . . .

(He smiles)

PHYLLIS Oh? What was I like?

BEN That was a long time ago. What kind of loving wife are you to drag me here?

PHYLLIS I think you wanted me to drag you.

BEN Any bets?

PHYLLIS I wanted to come back, Ben. One last look at where it all began. I've been devoting my attention to beginnings lately. I wanted something when I came here thirty years ago but I forgot to write it down and God knows what it was.

BEN Well, I'm glad you're glad to be here: that makes one of us.

(She laughs lightly, smiling as she crosses)

PHYLLIS I love the way you hate it when I'm happy and you're not.

(She makes her regal way to the wings and off. YOUNG PHYLLIS *follows her. More guests arrive. And more. And at the end, one final guest.*

His name is BUDDY PLUMMER. *He is an appealing, lively man of fifty-three. His sad-sweet face is wrinkled from years of too much smiling. He has been hurrying, and is clearly in a state of some anxiety: he can't stop talking and he can't stand still)*

BUDDY *(To no one in particular)* I'm one guy who hates to fly, and I've been flying all day long. *(Pausing, to one of the guests)* My wife, she took the early plane. You haven't seen her, have you? Blonde, about so high? *(The guest shakes his head.* BUDDY *smiles, shrugs and, turning to another guest, says)* It's crazy—all the traveling I do, I can't get used to flying. Once I met this fellow out in Denver—Salt Lake City. Anyway, he's in the airport bar and is he stoned. He's scared of planes, he tells me, so I say, "Look, fella, if it's that bad, miss the flight." "I can't," the guy says, "I'm the pilot." *(He looks hopefully for a smile, doesn't get one and turns back to the first guest)* She's a little girl and cute as hell, all kinds of flowers on her dress. You sure you haven't seen her?

(The guest shakes his head again, the music rises; there is sudden excited milling around. One of the scaffolding platforms moves downstage and on it, standing in a spotlight, is DIMITRI WEISMANN. *An acerbic, vital, energetic man, he must be eighty, though he looks no more than sixty-five)*

WEISMANN Welcome to our first and last reunion. For those of you whose memories may be going, I'm Dimitri Weismann. Every year, between the wars, I staged a Follies in this theater. Since then, this house has been a home to ballet, rep, movies, blue movies and now, in a final burst of glory, it's to be a parking lot. Before it goes, I felt an urge to see you one last time . . . a final chance to glamorize the old days, stumble through a song or two and lie about ourselves a little. I have, as you can see, spared no expense. Still there's a band, free food and drink, and the inevitable Roscoe, here as always to bring on the Weismann Girls. So take one last look at your girls. They won't be coming down these stairs again. I don't trust any music under thirty. Maestro, if you please!

(At which point ROSCOE—*an elderly tenor in top hat and tails—moves downstage center, strikes a majestic pose, opens his mouth and, in an absolutely gorgeous voice, begins to sing, accompanied by the four-piece onstage band)*

7

ROSCOE

Hats off,
Here they come, those
Beautiful girls.
That's what
You've been waiting for.

Nature never fashioned
A flower so fair.
No rose can compare—
Nothing respectable
Half so delectable.

Cheer them
In their glory,
Diamonds and pearls,
Dazzling jewels
By the score.

This is what beauty can be,
Beauty celestial, the best, you'll agree:
All for you,
These beautiful girls!

(*As the chorus ends,* ROSCOE *steps back, the music soars up as the full orchestra takes over and, high on a scaffolding platform, spotlights strike* CHRISTINE DONOVAN, *posed as she was thirty years ago, about to make her grand entrance down the Follies stairs. She wears, as all the ladies do, a sash on which her Follies year appears in gold.*

She smiles and starts down. One by one, all the ladies follow. Some are grand and sure, some flustered or self-conscious, some amused, some very serious. Years on their sashes range from 1918 to 1941. It feels almost as if an entire era, the time between the two great wars, were coming at us down the stairs.)

*Once down, the ladies parade across the stage, as they
originally did. As they move past us, everybody sings)*

ALL

Careful,
Here's the home of
Beautiful girls,
Where your
Reason is undone.

Beauty
Can't be hindered
From taking its toll.
You may lose control.
Faced with these Loreleis,
What man can moralize?

Caution,
On your guard with
Beautiful girls,
Flawless charmers
Every one.

This is how Samson was shorn:
Each in her style a Delilah reborn,
Each a gem,
A beautiful diadem
Of beautiful—welcome them—
These beautiful girls!

*(The line of girls across the stage breaks up the instant
the singing ends. There are shouted greetings and
squeals, hugs and kisses. WAITERS move about with trays
of drinks. SALLY, dazzled by the wonder of it all, is
standing, smiling, drinking it all in. She doesn't see
BUDDY as he comes up to her)*

9

BUDDY *(He hesitates a moment, as if uncertain what approach to take. Then, putting on a smile)* Hi, honey.

SALLY *(Startled, almost frightened, as she turns to him)* Buddy.

BUDDY That was great. You look sensational, I mean it, like a million bucks. How was your flight? You watch the movie?

SALLY Don't be angry with me, Buddy.

BUDDY It's O.K., we'll work it out.

SALLY I had to come, I wanted to so much.

BUDDY I know, I know you did. *(He smiles at her, touches her cheek. She anxiously returns the smile)* You're my girl, honey; just remember that.
(They go on talking briefly but we lose them in the hubbub. Excited little groups are forming; here and there, a couple starts to dance.

Throughout, the show moves rather like a film. All of the scaffolding platforms move forward and back, so that at one moment the stage is huge and empty and the next, closed in and intimate. And since no portion of the set holds anything specific, the action flows and drifts through space and time. Scenes shift as easily as cuts on film, and the material is free to be now here, now there or, on occasion, different places all at once.

As we lose BUDDY *and* SALLY *in the dancing, our attention shifts to* MAX *and* STELLA DEEMS, *who are talking with* WEISMANN. *In their middle-fifties,* MAX *and* STELLA *are a portly couple, moving with that special lightness heavy people sometimes have)*

STELLA DEEMS We had a hard time letting go. We kept on working all through '42. Then, one day—we were doing daytime radio in Boston—and Max, he turned to me and he said, "Stella, baby, this is a load of crap."

MAX DEEMS   The mike was open. Fifty thousand housewives heard the news.

STELLA DEEMS   Max didn't care. "I hate this lousy life," he said, and twenty minutes later we were on our way to Miami.

MAX DEEMS   She helps me in the store.

STELLA DEEMS   I do all my singing in the tub and, Mitya, it's the cat's pajamas.
       (*There is a little jump in time as the band, like a push-button radio, cuts from one dance tune to another, and we find* BEN *and* PHYLLIS *talking with* HATTIE WALKER, *an appealingly tough, no-nonsense lady in her mid-seventies*)

BEN (*As* HATTIE, *with some embarrassment, hands him a slip of paper and pencil*)   Nonsense, I'd be delighted. What's your grandson's name?

HATTIE WALKER   Jerome. He's just eleven, but he reads all your speeches.

BEN (*Chatting as he writes*)   A misspent youth. I spent mine in the local music hall. It had a broken fire door, and I saw every show that came to town. You wore a white dress cut to here. I didn't hear a note you sang. (*Handing it back to her with a charming smile*) Next time you find him reading, send him out to look for broken doors.

HATTIE WALKER   Mr. Stone, you sure know how to make a girl feel good.
       (*She moves away*)

PHYLLIS   My God, you're charming.

BEN   You should see me when you're not around.

PHYLLIS *(Eyes following one of the guests who is moving past)* They might've told us it was a costume party.
 (Our attention is caught by SOLANGE LA FITTE, *who is talking energetically to* WEISMANN. SOLANGE *is very French and very fashionable and very much alive at what she claims is sixty-six)*

SOLANGE LA FITTE Mitya, darling, it's me, Solange. I am a big success now. Lanvin, Guerlain, and now Solange. *(Producing a sample bottle from her evening bag, presenting it to him)* "Caveman" by Solange: for men who have an air about them. Vulgar but, my darling, it will change your life. I ask you, how is it possible to look like this at sixty-six? It's magic. *(Producing another sample from her bag)* "Magic" by Solange.
 (She gives WEISMANN *a hug and moves away)*

SALLY *(Looking about, excited and preoccupied, she sees* WEISMANN *a step away. A nervous figuration begins in the orchestra)* It's such a lovely party. I'm so glad I came.

WEISMANN *(He hasn't a clue who she is)* Of course, my dear.

SALLY It's me, it's Sally Durant, Mr. Weismann. I was in the mirror number.

WEISMANN *(Patting her hand. Either he used to lay her or he thinks he did)* Little Sally. Well, well, well . . .

SALLY *(Distracted, looking about as* WEISMANN *moves on to other guests)* That's Christine, isn't it? And there's Miss Deems and . . .
   (She sings)
   Ta da!
   Now, folks, we bring you,
   Di-rect from Phoenix,

Live and in person,
Sally Durant!
Here she is at last,
Twinkle in her eye—

PHYLLIS *(Coming upon her unexpectedly and unprepared. The
stage is empty; just the two of them)* Sally?
(As PHYLLIS *says,* "SALLY?" *we see* YOUNG PHYLLIS *and*
YOUNG SALLY *far upstage, in costume, racing down the
stairs.* SALLY *then, we sense at once, is much like* SALLY
now: gay, bubbling, pert, a little silly. PHYLLIS *is another
matter. The girl she was is open, vulnerable, emotional
and eager, and we get our first clear intimation of the
years of concentrated effort spent in turning a warm and
naive girl into a remote, sophisticated lady)*

YOUNG PHYLLIS
Sally! Sally, come on, will you?
That's our call.

YOUNG SALLY
Oh God, my hook's undone.

YOUNG PHYLLIS *(Moving to
help)* Let me.

YOUNG SALLY
O.K., O.K.
*(*YOUNG PHYLLIS *hooks it
up. The two girls look
at each other, giggle,
and impulsively throw
their arms around each
other)*

PHYLLIS Sally . . . *(*SALLY *looks at her blankly)* It is you, isn't
it?

13

SALLY *(Bright, full of energy)* Phyllis! Of course, it's me. You came, you're here. Just look at you. I want to hug you but I can't. You're like a queen, like Jackie Kennedy or something. What a thing to say. I'm talking silly.

PHYLLIS *(Controlled, cool, graceful, barely touching SALLY as she hugs her)* If you can't, I can.
   (As PHYLLIS and SALLY embrace, YOUNG PHYLLIS and YOUNG SALLY separate and race upstage)

YOUNG PHYLLIS
Hurry, hurry!

SALLY *(As the memory fades)* It's just that out in Phoenix nothing like this ever happens. I don't think I've slept for days, I'm so excited.

PHYLLIS *(Stepping slightly back)* Sally, you look just as cute as ever.

SALLY Me? Oh, I'm a mess. I've got a tummy and my hair's too bleached. Who cares? New York's all changed. I couldn't even find the theater tonight, and this afternoon when I walked past 44th and Third—why, Phyl, it wasn't there.

PHYLLIS What wasn't?

SALLY Our apartment, where we lived. Don't you remember? Five flights up. I did the cleaning and you cooked: baked beans and peanut butter sandwiches.

PHYLLIS You never made the beds.

SALLY I still don't. And that awful bathtub in the kitchen, and the racket when the El went by.

PHYLLIS *(A bit surprised)* You know, I think I loved it.

SALLY You were homesick and you cried a lot but we had fun.

PHYLLIS You married Buddy, didn't you?

SALLY *(Nodding happily)* He always liked you, Phyl.

PHYLLIS I liked him, too.

SALLY You married Ben. I know. I read about you in the magazines. I even saw your living room in *Vogue*. It's blue. Is Ben still in Europe?

PHYLLIS He's not with the U.N. any more. He's here now.

SALLY Here? Tonight? Phyl, tell me something?

PHYLLIS If I can.
(They exit together as HATTIE WALKER *comes out of the crowd upstage. She speaks as if to someone, but is alone)*

HATTIE WALKER *(Kind and sympathetic)* . . . yes, yes, I know. It's always sad to lose a husband. I've lost five. You wouldn't think it now, to look at me. I always married crazy boys. They raced around in motor cars and aeroplanes. They lived too fast, but while they lived, my goodness, it was something.
(Our attention jumps to BEN *and* BUDDY, *seated on some rubble to one side of the stage. They have drinks in their hands and seem casual and friendly)*

BUDDY Sure, I think about the past. A lot, I guess. Don't you?

BEN There's not much to think about.

BUDDY I haven't read your book on Wilson yet. Sally bought a copy, though. We keep it on the coffee table.

BEN Just the place.

BUDDY   I always knew you'd make it big.

BEN   I had a lot of luck.

BUDDY   How's life with you and Phyllis?

BEN   She's an extraordinary woman, endlessly exciting.
(YOUNG BUDDY *and* YOUNG BEN *appear. They are walking down a street on their way to class*)

> YOUNG BUDDY
> I got you a terrific date to-night.

> YOUNG BEN
> I can't. I've got a class.

> YOUNG BUDDY
> Aw, come on, Ben. It's all fixed up. She's Sally's room-mate.

> YOUNG BEN *(With a shrug)* I don't know.

> YOUNG BUDDY
> Her name is Phyllis something.

> YOUNG BEN
> What's she like?

> YOUNG BUDDY
> Nice girl. She's lonely. Do the kid a favor. Whatcha got to lose?

BUDDY *(As the memory fades)* I've been lucky, too. I mean, you grow up hearing it's the little things that count, and

you know what? It's true. I come home and I'm welcome.
I see Sally and I'm glad to see her. No big deal, no fireworks
—I'm sentimental on my second drink. You ever play
around?

BEN I gave all that up years ago.

BUDDY Same here. Not like the old days, is it? Law School:
who could study? I'd have made some lousy lawyer. No
regrets; right, Ben? *(A beautiful young* WAITRESS, *tray in
hand, moves briskly by, upstage.* BUDDY *turns, devours her with
his eyes)* Hey, will you look at that.
(He grins at BEN, *turns and follows the* WAITRESS *off. As
he goes, the band cuts to new music and* VINCENT *and*
VANESSA *dance into view. Tall, supple, graceful, close to
sixty, they are unmistakably a dance team)*

VINCENT *(Speaking to no one)* We retired years ago.

VANESSA We played the clubs a while but after dancing in
the Follies . . .
(She shrugs)

VINCENT So we bought ourselves an Arthur Murray fran-
chise.

VANESSA Sounds hokey but we keep in shape.

VINCENT Styles change. You never know.
(Our attention shifts to another area where we find HEIDI
SCHILLER. *In her eighties, she stands tall and queenly,
dressed in white lace, her hand on the arm of her
uniformed* CHAUFFEUR)

HEIDI SCHILLER *(In a soft Viennese accent)* It's my waltz
they're playing. Franz Lehar wrote it for me in Vienna.
I was having coffee in my drawing room—in ran Franz

and straight to the piano. "Liebchen, it's for you." Or was it Oscar Straus? Facts never interest me. What matters is the song.

(Our attention shifts again, this time to BEN *as he turns and sees* CARLOTTA CAMPION. CARLOTTA *is a one-time movie star and in terrific shape for fifty. She is the kind of woman who not only has seen everything but has liked the look of it)*

CARLOTTA *(With a laugh of happy recognition)* Ben Stone!

BEN Well, it's not much of a ball to be belle of, but congratulations anyway. That outfit is a triumph of restraint.

CARLOTTA I always liked the way you talk. I haven't seen your picture in the papers lately.

BEN Thanks, the same to you.

CARLOTTA You ought to watch more television. I've got a series of my own. You still in politics?

BEN I said the wrong things. Now I'm president of a foundation.

(CARLOTTA laughs and drifts off. BEN is left alone. Far upstage, couples are dancing. SALLY emerges from them, moves downstage, sees BEN. She gasps and stops. Then, after a beat)

SALLY Ben?

(As SALLY says, "Ben?" we see YOUNG SALLY. She wears a street coat and is all alone. Eyes blazing with outrage, she moves to BEN)

YOUNG SALLY

Ben. Ben Stone, I want a reason. Look at me. Damn it,

you turn around and look at
me.

(The memory goes as
SALLY *starts to sing)*

SALLY   Ben, it's me.
(She sings)
Now, folks, we bring you
Di-rect from Phoenix,
Live and in person,
Sally Durant!
Here she is at last,
Twinkle in her eye,
Hot off the press,
Strictly a mess,
Nevertheless . . .
(Smiling nervously)
Hi, Ben . . .
(Then, before he can respond)
No, don't look at me—
Please, not just yet.
Why am I here? This is crazy!
No, don't look at me—
I know that face,
You're trying to place
The name . . .
Say something, Ben, anything.
No, don't talk to me.
Ben, I forget:
What were we like, it's so hazy!
Look at these people,
Aren't they eerie?
Look at this party,

Isn't it dreary?
I'm so glad I came.
   (Music continues under)

BEN *(Looking at her)* Can I look now? *(She nods, smiling nervously. With great seriousness)* Yes, it's possible. You might be Sally. Did you fall asleep at Toscanini broadcasts? *(She nods)* Did you eat Baby Ruths for breakfast?

SALLY I still do sometimes. Oh, Ben, you're just the way I knew you'd be. You make me feel like I was nineteen and the four of us were going on the town.

BEN and SALLY *(After a pause, sing)*
   So—
   Just look at us . . .

SALLY
   Fat . . .

BEN

   Turning gray . . .

BEN and SALLY
   Still playing games,
   Acting crazy.

SALLY
   Isn't it awful?

BEN

   God, how depressing—

BEN and SALLY
   Me, I'm a hundred,
   You, you're a blessing—
   I'm so glad I came!

BEN *(Speaks)* What we need is a drink.

(The song ends as BEN *throws a casual arm around* SALLY *and the two of them move through the scaffolding and out of view.*

As they go, the onstage band strikes up something bright and half a dozen couples appear from nowhere, dancing vigorously.

CARLOTTA CAMPION *moves slowly through the dancers, as if she were in some other place, listening to some other music)*

CARLOTTA *(Struck by a thought; she smiles wryly)* I never get to talk. I take a plane, go to a party, every guy I meet says, "Boy, oh boy, a real live movie actress; tell me all about yourself." I get as far as "I was born in Idaho" and he starts telling me the story of his life. Not just his troubles: he unloads the whole thing, ups and downs. Mostly, he just wants to talk. Sometimes, he wants a place to put his head awhile. Other times, he wants the works; some nights, he gets it. You want to hear the story of my life?

(Our attention shifts to BUDDY *and* PHYLLIS, *dancing on a platform high upstage)*

PHYLLIS *(Interrupts him with a laugh)* I didn't do that, Buddy, did I?

BUDDY Cross my heart. In Central Park. You and Sally both dove in. We dared you to.

PHYLLIS Oh, Buddy, it's so good to see you—*(She gives him an impulsive squeeze)*—and what fun it was to do things. We don't do things any more; we say them. *(Across from them,* BEN *and* SALLY *stop dancing, stand and talk)* Our life is like a sound track; words and words with all the action missing. Why, do you know we've even got a chauffeur who's articulate?

21

(BEN *and* SALLY *stroll a few steps.* BUDDY *and* PHYLLIS *continue talking inaudibly*)

SALLY   . . . and Phyl: she's even lovelier than ever, and the way she talks now, goodness, like she had her thinking-cap on all the time. I feel so empty-headed. Always did, I guess. The way she used to look at me. She's much too lovely just to say, "I think you're dumb" or something. She was right, though. You should see my checkbook, it's like—Oh, dear Lord, I'm boring you.

BEN   *(Smiling, enjoying her)*   I didn't think it showed.
    (They sit on the steps and go on talking, silently now. Save for the two couples, the stage is empty)

BUDDY   Ben looks terrific. Kept his hair and everything. Me, I'm in oil these days. It sounds big but it isn't. I'm a salesman and we sell these rigs and drills and I'm away a lot. I'm good at selling. I like meeting people, going places; keeps the juices flowing. *(Looking around)* God, the time we clocked here, me and Ben; the things we all did. You remember?

PHYLLIS   I don't know. *(She shrugs)* I guess I make a point of not remembering.

BUDDY   *(Coming down a flight of stairs, out to the stage)*   I wish I could. Sometimes it even seems a little nuts to me. I mean, just look around you: stage door, call board— what's so special? And some days, I'll sit for hours, seeing it so clear . . . *(Interrupting himself, looking around, his manner increasingly feverish)* Ben and me, that's where we used to sit. The place was packed with guys and flowers, waiting for the girls to come down.

> YOUNG BUDDY'S VOICE   *(Faint and eerie, singing)*
> Hey, up there . . .

BUDDY You always took your sweet time getting ready, so we'd josh around, tell jokes. I even carved my name here someplace.

> YOUNG BUDDY'S VOICE
> Way up there . . .
>
> YOUNG BUDDY and BUDDY
> Whaddaya say, up there?

BUDDY This place gives me the creeps. I keep on thinking —Phyl, don't think I'm nuts, but being back together here, the four of us, I feel all the things I used to feel. Like it was yesterday.

PHYLLIS *(Fondly, sitting on the stairs)* Oh, Buddy, that's a million years ago. Forget it. 1941? When I see pictures of myself back then, I think, "Somebody's put a stranger in my scrapbook."

BEN *(Animatedly as he and* SALLY *come down a flight of stairs and join* BUDDY *and* PHYLLIS*)* . . . but I can't have. I don't like corsages.

SALLY Every night you'd bring one.

PHYLLIS Yesterday's gardenias, darling; always wilted.

BUDDY Sure, we got them from the lady on the corner. They were cheaper there.

BEN *(Remembering, shaking his head, amused)* The things I did.

SALLY And then we'd go and dance all night at Tommy's.

BUDDY Tony's.

BEN Tony's. Well, my God.

SALLY Don't you wish you were still young, Ben?

BEN Once was bad enough. I wouldn't want to face all that again.

BUDDY *(Singing up to the flies)*
  Hey, up there!
  Way up there!
  Whaddaya say, up there?
    (Speaking, strains of music flowing through the speech)
  I see it all.
  It's like a movie in my head that plays and plays.
  It isn't just the bad things I remember. It's the whole show.
    (Singing)
  Waiting around for the girls upstairs
  After the curtain came down,
  Money in my pocket to spend,
  "Honey, could you maybe get a friend for my friend?"

BEN
  Hearing the sound of the girls above
  Dressing to go on the town,

BUDDY
  Clicking heels on steel and cement,

BEN
  Picking up the giggles floating down through the vent,

BEN and BUDDY
  Goddamnedest hours that I ever spent
  We're waiting for the girls
  Upstairs.

BUDDY
  Hey, up there!
  Way up there!
  Whaddaya say, up there?

BEN *(Pointing things out, starting to get excited)*
    That's where the keys hung and
    That's where you picked up your mail.

BUDDY
    I remember:
    Me and Ben,
    Me and Ben,
    We'd come around at ten,
    Me and Ben,
    And hang around the wings
    Watching things
    With what-the-hell-was-his-name,
    You know, the old guy . . .
    Max! I remember . . .

    Anyway,
    There we'd stay
    Until the curtain fell.
    And when the curtain fell,
    Then all hell broke:
    Girls on the run
    And scenery flying,
    Doors slamming left and right.

BEN
    Girls in their un-
    Dies, blushing but trying
    Not to duck out of sight.

BEN and BUDDY
    Girls by the hun-
    Dreds waving and crying,
    "See you tomorrow night!"
    Girls looking frazzled and girls looking great,
    Girls in a frenzy to get to a date,

Girls like a madhouse and two of them late . . .
And who had to wait?
And wait . . .
And wait . . .

PHYLLIS

Waiting around for the boys downstairs,
Stalling as long as we dare.
Which dress from my wardrobe of two?
(One of them was borrowed and the other was blue.)

SALLY

Holding our ground for the boys below,
Fussing around with our hair,

PHYLLIS

Giggling, wriggling out of our tights,

SALLY

Chattering and clattering down all of those flights—

SALLY and PHYLLIS

God, I'd forgotten there ever were nights
Of waiting for the boys
Downstairs.

BUDDY

You up there!

SALLY

Down in a minute!

BEN

You two up there!

PHYLLIS

Just keep your shirts on!

BEN and BUDDY
    Aren't you through up there?

SALLY and PHYLLIS
    Heard you the first time!

BEN and BUDDY	SALLY and PHYLLIS
Look, are you coming or	
Aren't you coming 'cause	Coming, we're coming, will
Look, if we're going, we	You hold your horses, we're
Gotta get going 'cause	Coming, we're ready, be
Look, they won't hold us	There in a jiffy, we're
A table at ringside all	Coming, we're coming. All
Night!	Right!

(And suddenly, as if the force of their collective memories had summoned them, YOUNG PHYLLIS *and* YOUNG SALLY *come racing across a high platform and down the stairs as, from the shadows,* YOUNG BUDDY *and* YOUNG BEN *appear. All four of them are happy and excited, dressed up for a big date on the town. The music pulses under as they speak)*

YOUNG SALLY *(Cute as a button)*
Hi.

YOUNG BEN
Girls.

YOUNG PHYLLIS *(She adores him)* Ben.

YOUNG BUDDY
Sally.

(As the young selves start to sing, BEN, PHYLLIS, BUDDY *and* SALLY

27

*stand close to them, see-
ing them; not directly
but rather as if the mem-
ories were some place
in their minds. They are
rapt, caught up; now
one and now another
sings a phrase, a word or
two along with the
memories)*

YOUNG SALLY

Boy, we're beat.

YOUNG BUDDY

You look neat.

YOUNG PHYLLIS

We saw you in the
wings.

YOUNG BEN

How are things?

YOUNG PHYLLIS

Did someone pass you
in?

YOUNG BUDDY

Slipped a fin
To   what-the-hell-is-his-
name,
You know, the doorman.

YOUNG PHYLLIS

Al?

YOUNG BUDDY

No.

YOUNG SALLY

Big?

YOUNG BEN

Fat.

YOUNG PHYLLIS

Young?

YOUNG BUDDY

Bald.

YOUNG SALLY

Harry.

YOUNG BEN

Yeah.

YOUNG SALLY

Okey-doaks.

YOUNG BUDDY

Come on, folks.

YOUNG PHYLLIS

And where we gonna
go?

YOUNG BEN

A little joint I know—

YOUNG SALLY

What?

YOUNG BUDDY

Great new show there.

YOUNG PHYLLIS

Hey, I thought you said
tonight'd be Tony's—

YOUNG BUDDY
This joint is just as grand.

YOUNG SALLY
We girls got dressed for dancing at Tony's—

YOUNG BEN
This joint is in demand.

YOUNG SALLY and YOUNG PHYLLIS
Ta-ta, goodbye, you'll find us at Tony's—

YOUNG BUDDY and YOUNG BEN
Wait till you hear the band!

YOUNG SALLY and YOUNG PHYLLIS
You told us Tony's,
That we'd go to Tony's.
Then Ben mentioned Tony's
Well, someone said Tony's.

There's dancing at Tony's—
All right, then, we'll go!

YOUNG BUDDY and YOUNG BEN

I told you Tony's?
I never said Tony's.

When's Ben mentioned Tony's?
It's ritzy at Tony's—
All right, then, we'll go!

(*And, as suddenly as they appeared, the memories are gone.* BEN, PHYLLIS, BUDDY *and* SALLY *stand quite still for a moment, caught by the remembered joy of being young. Then, as the music pulses on, they snap back to the present, look at one another, then away, all deeply shaken by the immediacy of the past and by regret for what's been lost and wasted. Angrily at first, they turn toward us and sing*)

BUDDY

Waiting around for the girls upstairs,
Weren't we chuckleheads then?

BEN

Very young and very old hat—
Everybody has to go through stages like that.

SALLY, PHYLLIS, BEN and BUDDY

Waiting around for the girls upstairs—
Thank you but never again.
Life was fun, but oh, so intense.
Everything was possible and nothing made sense
Back there when one of the major events
Was waiting for the girls,
Waiting for the girls,
Waiting for the girls
Upstairs.

> (*The stage goes dark. Flash bulbs explode. The lights rise to bright as the party spills over the stage; laughter, noise and general gaiety.* BEN, PHYLLIS, BUDDY *and* SALLY *splinter off in different directions through the tide of guests.*
> WILLY WHEELER, *sixtyish and portly, does a cartwheel for a* PHOTOGRAPHER)

WILLY WHEELER   I keep my hand in. I keep working.

> (*We move to* EMILY *and* THEODORE WHITMAN, *who are posing for a photo with* WEISMANN *on a flight of stairs. The Whitmans are a tiny, bright, papery couple in their seventies*)

EMILY WHITMAN   We met at an audition. Teddy was a dough-boy, weren't you, dear? You'd just come back from France and when we danced, my blouse kept getting stuck on all your medals.

THEODORE WHITMAN   Emmy, that's an act we did.

EMILY WHITMAN Why, so it was. But acts are real, they happen, and I met you, didn't I?

PHOTOGRAPHER *(To a group of ladies)* All right, ladies! Line up, please. Now, hold it, ladies!
(And our eyes go to another area, where WEISMANN *is talking to a beautiful young* WAITRESS*)*

WEISMANN They seem absurd to you, no doubt. They do to me. They look back at their life here and see it as a golden time: bugle beads and peacock feathers. Girls like you, they waited for me in my office, on the stairs, around the corner, anything to see me. And for what? To be a Weismann Girl. And I could have them for a smile. *(Smiling at the* WAITRESS*)* You want to be a star, my dear?
(And suddenly, the stage is clear and dark except for EMILY *and* THEODORE WHITMAN, *who stand in a spotlight looking at us as if they were about to speak. Instead of speaking, they burst into song)*

EMILY and THEODORE WHITMAN
    Listen to the rain on the roof go
    Pit-pitty-pat
    Pit-pitty-pat-pitty,
    Sit, kitty cat,
    We won't get home for hours.
    Relax and
    Listen to the rain on the roof go
    Plunk-planka-plink
    Plunk-planka-plink-planka,
    Let's have a drink
    And shelter from the showers.

    Rain, rain, don't go away,
    Fill up the sky.

Rain through the night,
We'll stay
Cozy and dry.

Listen to the rain on the roof go
Pit-pitty-pat
    (They kiss)
Plunk-a-plink
    (They kiss)
Plank
    (They kiss)
Pity that
It's not a hurricane.
Listen plink to the
    (Kiss. Kiss)
Lovely rain.
    *(The number goes as quickly as it came, almost as if it
    never happened. The Whitmans stand immobile at one
    side of the stage as* SOLANGE LA FITTE *comes toward us out
    of the darkness)*

SOLANGE LA FITTE *(She sings)*
New York has neon, Berlin has bars,
But ah! Paris!
Shanghai has silk and Madrid guitars,
But ah! Paris!
In Cairo you find bizarre bazaars,
In London pip! pip! you sip tea.
But when it comes to love,
None of the above
Compares, *compris?*
So if it's making love
That you're thinking of,
Ah ah ah ah ah ah ah ah ah! Paris!

I have seen the ruins of Rome,
I've been in the igloos of Nome.
I have gone to Moscow,
It's very gay—
Well, anyway,
On the first of May!
I have seen Rangoon and Soho,
And I like them more than so-so.
But when there's a moon,
Goodbye Rangoon,
Hello, Montmartre, hello!

Peking has rickshaws, New Orleans jazz,
But ah! Paris!
Beirut has sunshine—that's all it has,
But ah! Paris!
Constantinople has Turkish baths
And Athens that lovely debris.
Carlsbad may have a spa,
But for ooh-la-la,
You come with me!
Carlsbad is where you're cured
After you have toured
Ah ah ah ah ah ah ah ah ah! Paris!

(SOLANGE *stands motionless, arms outflung, opposite the*
Whitmans as HATTIE WALKER *strides out of the shadows*
and into a spotlight)

HATTIE WALKER *(She sets herself, looks at us with a steely eye,*
takes a deep breath and belts out)
I'm just a
Broadway Baby,
Walking off my tired feet,
Pounding Forty-second Street
To be in a show.

Broadway Baby,
Learning how to sing and dance,
Waiting for that one big chance
To be in a show.

Gee,
I'd like to be
On some marquee,
All twinkling lights,
A spark
To pierce the dark
From Battery Park
To Washington Heights.
Some day, maybe,
All my dreams will be repaid:
Hell, I'd even play the maid
To be in a show.

Say, Mr. Producer,
I'm talking to you, sir:
I don't need a lot,
Only what I got,
Plus a tube of greasepaint and a follow-spot!

I'm just a Broadway Baby,
Slaving at a five-and-ten,
Dreaming of the great day when
I'll be in a show.
Broadway Baby,
Making rounds all afternoon,
Eating at a greasy spoon
To save on my dough.

At
My tiny flat
There's just my cat,

A bed and a chair.
Still
I'll stick it till
I'm on a bill
All over Times Square.

(Spotlights return to the Whitmans and SOLANGE *as they come to life and join* HATTIE, *all three songs pounding out at once)*

HATTIE	SOLANGE	THE WHITMANS
Broadway Baby,	New York has neon,	Listen to the rain
Walking off my tired feet,	Berlin has bars, But ah! Paris!	on the roof go Pit-pitty-pat
Pounding Forty-second Street	Shanghai has silk and Madrid guitars	Pit-pitty-pat-pitty, Sit, kitty cat,
To be in a show	But ah! Paris!	You won't get home for hours.
Broadway Baby,	In Cairo you find bizarre bazaars	Relax and
Learning how to sing and dance,	In London pip! pip! you sip tea	Listen to the rain on the roof go
	Ah ah ah ah ah!	Plunk-planka-plink Plunk-planka-plink-planka
		(Kiss. Kiss)
		Lovely
	Ah ah ah ah ah!	

Working for a nice man
Like a Ziegfeld or a
  Weismann in a

Great big	Ah ah ah ah ah ah!	Listen to the
Broadway show!	Ah ah ah! Paris!	Lovely rain!

(The number builds to a shameless climax and ends with a blackout. Pale lights rise. The ghost of a SHOWGIRL, *tall*

"Who's That Woman?" with Sheila Smith as
MEREDITH LANE, Ethel Barrymore Colt as CHRISTINE
DONOVAN, Alexis Smith as PHYLLIS, Dorothy Collins as
SALLY, Helon Blount as DEEDEE WEST and Yvonne de Carlo
as CARLOTTA CAMPION, mirrored by their former
selves in the background.

and all in white, moves languidly across the empty stage
as BEN *and* SALLY *enter. They have been having a pleasant*
time and she is chattering away)

SALLY Your life must be so glamorous.

BEN I'll bet you think champagne is glamorous.

SALLY Well, isn't it, and all the famous people and the
parties?

BEN Oh, yes. The statesmen talk about the servant problem and the writers talk about their picture deals and the
opera singers, all they talk about is food.

SALLY Honestly?

BEN Would I lie to you? No, it's a good life, really. Success.
All it really is is doing what you want to do. It's possible
to be a jolly farmer: different men need different things.
It's knowing what you want, that's the secret.
   (He sings)
You're either a poet
Or you're a lover
Or you're the famous
Benjamin Stone.
You take one road,
You try one door,
There isn't time for any more.
One's life consists of either/or.
One has regrets
Which one forgets,
And as the years go on,
The road you didn't take
Hardly comes to mind,
Does it?
The door you didn't try,

37

Where could it have led?
The choice you didn't make
Never was defined,
Was it?
Dreams you didn't dare
Are dead.
Were they ever there?
Who said?
I don't remember,
I don't remember
At all.

(He stops, stands still, remembering. As the music spins on, we see YOUNG BEN *and* YOUNG BUDDY. *They are walking along a street.* YOUNG BEN *is dressed up for a date)*

YOUNG BUDDY *(Handing a set of keys to* YOUNG BEN*)* Here you are. Keys to the old jalopy.

YOUNG BEN

Thanks.

YOUNG BUDDY *(Taking out his wallet)* You need a couple of bucks?

YOUNG BEN

I'm fine.

YOUNG BUDDY

Come on, it's only money, what's it matter?

YOUNG BEN *(Sitting, looking into his future as* YOUNG BUDDY *strolls off)* You wouldn't know.

BEN *(Disturbed, shaking himself out of it)*
The books I'll never read
Wouldn't change a thing,
Would they?
The girls I'll never know
I'm too tired for.
The lives I'll never lead
Couldn't make me sing,
Could they? Could they? Could they?
Chances that you miss,
Ignore.
Ignorance is bliss—
What's more,
You won't remember,
You won't remember
At all,
Not at all.

    (BEN *stands in anguish as the music churns on.* YOUNG
    PHYLLIS *appears high on a platform, looks lovingly down
    at* YOUNG BEN, *who is jangling Buddy's car keys)*

                    YOUNG BEN
                Borrowed money, borrowed
                car. Some day I'm going to
                have the biggest goddamn
                limousine.

                    YOUNG PHYLLIS
                We've got each other, Ben.
                What difference does it make?

                    YOUNG BEN
                All the difference.

                    (YOUNG PHYLLIS *fades
                    away, and it is a much
                    disturbed Ben who
                    sings)*

BEN

You yearn for the women,
Long for the money,
Envy the famous
Benjamin Stones.
You take your road,
The decades fly,
The yearnings fade, the longings die.
You learn to bid them all goodbye.
And oh, the peace,
The blessed peace . . .
At last you come to know:
The roads you never take
Go through rocky ground,
Don't they?
The choices that you make
Aren't all that grim.
The worlds you never see
Still will be around,
Won't they?
The Ben I'll never be,
Who remembers him?

> (*The number ends as* BEN *stares into space.* BUDDY *and* PHYLLIS *appear upstage, and look down on* BEN *and* SALLY)

SALLY *I* remember him. I even think I loved him once. (*She takes* BEN *by the hand, and moves with him to join the dancing*)

BUDDY (*Looking at* SALLY *and* BEN) They make a lovely couple. What's wrong with me tonight?

PHYLLIS You got the shakes?

BUDDY *(Drinking)* Not me; I'm on the wagon. You got any kids, Phyl?

PHYLLIS None at all. Ben put it off, and then it was too late.

BUDDY We've got two: Tom and Tim. Sally picked the names out. They're in San Francisco now and she gets lonely for them, so she calls them on the phone and fights. She's fought with everyone she knows. It's crazy. Phyl, all I want is Sally back the way she used to be. I want the girl I married.

PHYLLIS *(Wryly)* That's impossible but never mind.

BUDDY I told her not to come tonight. She's forty-nine, Phyl, and she ran away from home to be with Ben.

PHYLLIS Oh, that's absurd.

BUDDY It's happening again, just like I knew it would.

PHYLLIS What is?

BUDDY She's still in love with Ben.

PHYLLIS I used to wonder but I never knew for sure. Times change. It might have mattered once.
(And YOUNG PHYLLIS *and* YOUNG BEN *come strolling slowly by.* PHYLLIS, *caught by surprise at the sweetness of her memory, watch as* YOUNG PHYLLIS *looks wide-eyed at the engagement ring* YOUNG BEN *has just given her)*

> YOUNG PHYLLIS
> Oh, Ben, I said and said it cost too much.

> YOUNG BEN
> It's only half a carat.
> YOUNG PHYLLIS
> It's so beautiful.

YOUNG BEN

You'll make a good wife,
Phyl.

YOUNG PHYLLIS

I'll try. Oh, Ben, I'll try so
hard, I'll study and I'll read—
I'm not much now, I know
that—and I'll walk my feet
off in the Metropolitan Museum . . .

> *(They stroll arm in arm
> into the shadows;* PHYL-
> LIS *is close to anger as
> she shakes away the
> memory)*

PHYLLIS Bargains, Buddy. That's the way to get through.
One makes bargains with one's life. That's what maturity
amounts to. When we're young and every road looks
clear, we take them all, ignoring Newton's laws of motion, going every way at once. Star, mother, hostess,
hausfrau. So I learned to be an artist with my life. I
constantly select, as if each day were a painting and I had
to get the colors right. We're careful of our colors, Ben
and I, and what we've made is beautiful. I had a lover
once. His name was Jack, I think. He played the drums
and had long hair and no command of language. He was
young and crude and foolish, and we'd wash away the
afternoons with Gallo wine and one another, listening to
the pop hits and the news. I have a birthmark under my
left breast, just here—my only flaw. I think he loved that
in me most of all. He was so tender touching it, and when
he kissed me there, one found it difficult to breathe. I
thought it answered everything, but these things pass,

and I have thirty thousand dollars worth of Georgian silver in my dining room.

BUDDY What happened to you, Phyl? Where did you go?

PHYLLIS *(Eyes bright, upset and angry)* I went my own damn way, and don't make waves.

> *(She turns and strides away. Upstage, there has been quiet social dancing. Out of this now, VINCENT and VANESSA come. The music eases into a tango, and they start to dance an old routine.*
>
> *As they dance, YOUNG VINCENT and YOUNG VANESSA materialize from the shadows and dance along with them. Upstage, three ghostly couples, also part of the original number, join the dance. It is a lush, romantic number, and we watch the differences, both great and small, that thirty years have made.*
>
> *The number ends in darkness, and when lights return, we see BEN and SALLY chatting in a corner of an empty stage)*

SALLY . . . and then the Follies closed—I never missed it, Ben, not really.

BEN Neither did the audience.

SALLY I know. And after that we had Tom, and then Tim came along, and when the war was over, Buddy couldn't wait to start in making money. We've lived every place you can imagine, Ben. The Sunshine City, that's Detroit —or is it Houston? Anyway, we've lived in both, and New Orleans—it really is romantic—and Los Angeles—

BEN Getting there is half the fun.

SALLY We're out in Phoenix now. We've got this huge old house. Oh, it's a different life from yours, you wouldn't

like it—but you're right, it's fun. Can you imagine it, at
my age, having fun? But most of all, what makes my life
so good is Buddy.

(She sings)
Life is slow but it seems exciting
'Cause Buddy's there.
Gourmet cooking and letter writing
And knowing Buddy's there.
Every morning—don't faint—
I tend the flowers. Can you believe it?
Every weekend, I paint
For umpteen hours.
And, yes, I miss a lot
Living like a shut-in.
No, I haven't got
Cooks and cars and diamonds.
Yes, my clothes are not
Paris fashions, but in
Buddy's eyes,
I'm young, I'm beautiful.
In Buddy's eyes
I don't get older.
So life is ducky
And time goes flying
And I'm so lucky
I feel like crying,
And . . .

(SALLY's *voice catches as she is swept by memory.* YOUNG
SALLY, *hurt and much upset, comes rushing by.* YOUNG
BEN *follows her)*

YOUNG BEN *(Calls out)* Sally.
Wait.

(She stops)

YOUNG SALLY
We're finished, Ben. I mean
it.

YOUNG BEN
Hey, come on, come on.

YOUNG SALLY *(Turning on him
the moment he touches her)*
You give a ring to her and
mess around with me. Ben,
you can't play with people's
feelings, you can't treat me like
that.

YOUNG BEN
O.K. . . . if that's the way you
feel . . .

YOUNG SALLY
Damn you, you know the way
I feel. *(Going into his arms)*
Oh God, Ben . . .
 *(Arms tight about each
 other, passing close to
 *SALLY, they drift off.
 She watches them a
 beat, then tears her
 eyes away and turns to*
 BEN *and, smiling, con-
 tinues singing)*

SALLY
In Buddy's eyes,
I'm young, I'm beautiful.
In Buddy's eyes,

I can't get older.
I'm still the princess,
Still the prize.
In Buddy's eyes,
I'm young, I'm beautiful.
In Buddy's arms,
On Buddy's shoulder,
I won't get older.
Nothing dies.
And all I ever dreamed I'd be,
The best I ever thought of me,
Is every minute there to see
In Buddy's eyes.

(*The song ends. They are very close together. The on-stage band strikes up a tune. Wordlessly, they put their arms around each other and begin to dance. As they do, PHYLLIS sweeps onstage. She cuts in, tapping BEN politely on the shoulder. Then, smiling, she takes SALLY by the hand and leads her to a corner*)

PHYLLIS (*As they sit*) Let's dish. I can't wait, tell me everything. You ever miss New York?

SALLY (*With a shrug and a smile*) It's changed so much.

PHYLLIS It grows on you: you get to like hostility and filth and rotten manners. Tell me more. Who made your dress or did you make it? What's the weather out in Phoenix? How do you like my husband?

SALLY Ben? I've always liked him: you know that.

PHYLLIS How was his conversation? Did he sparkle for you?

SALLY We just talked about old times and little things.

PHYLLIS You find him changed?

SALLY Not really, not down deep.

PHYLLIS I rarely dip beneath the surface. Is his heart still young?

SALLY You know it is, Phyl. You don't have to ask me.

PHYLLIS Buddy thinks you're still in love with him.

SALLY *(Isn't Buddy sweet?)* That man; he gets so jealous sometimes.
(We hear the onstage band begin to play "Who's That Woman?")

PHYLLIS What of? That's the enigma of the week.

SALLY I'm sorry, I don't want to fight with you, Phyl. I don't have to.

PHYLLIS Well, now, there's a riveting remark. Would you care to expand on that?

STELLA DEEMS *(Entering)* I'm not making an ass out of myself alone. I do it, we all do it.
(One after another, the girls originally in the number appear from different parts of the stage and, moving briskly downstage center, take up their old positions in the chorus line)

DEEDEE WEST Would you believe it? I've got stage fright.

SALLY *(Starting to join them, turning back to* PHYLLIS*)* Well, aren't you coming?

PHYLLIS If you can, I can.

MEREDITH LANE This number winded me when I was nineteen.

SALLY I wish we had our old costumes on.

CHRISTINE DONOVAN I haven't danced in thirty years.

SALLY Phyl, do you remember?

PHYLLIS *(Taking up her position, posing)* I remember.
(They all line up behind STELLA DEEMS*)*

STELLA DEEMS Well, heaven help us. *(To the band leader)* Hit
it, baby.
> *(The band starts to vamp.* STELLA *throws her head back
> and sails into the number. Her voice is still terrific, but
> she gets a little winded from the moves)*
Who's that woman? I know her well,
All decked out head to toe.
She lives life like a carousel:
Beau after beau after beau.
Nightly, daily,
Always laughing gaily,
Seems I see her everywhere I go.
Oh—

Who's that woman?
I know I know that woman,
So clever, but ever so sad.
Love, she said, was a fad.
The kind of love that she couldn't make fun of
She'd have none of.
Who's that woman,
That cheery, weary woman
Who's dressing for yet one more spree?
Each day I see her pass
In my looking-glass—
Lord, Lord, Lord, that woman is me!

SALLY, PHYLLIS, CARLOTTA, CHRISTINE, DEEDEE and MEREDITH
Mirror, mirror, on the wall,
Who's the saddest gal in town?
Who's been riding for a fall?
Whose Lothario let her down?
Mirror, mirror, answer me:
Who is she who plays the clown?
Is she out each night till three?
Does she laugh with too much glee?
On reflection, she'd agree.
Mirror, mirror,
Mirror, mirror,
Mirror, mirror . . .

(STELLA *struts off to the wings, and the "Chorus Girls,"
their singing ended, begin to dance in earnest. They remember their moves remarkably well, and enjoy them-
selves as they manage to get through their attitudes and
high kicks.*

*Then the music slows, the "Chorus Girls" form a
line across the stage and, unmistakably, it's time to tap-
dance. It begins. We hear the taps and, looking upstage
in the dimness, we see all six memories—*YOUNG PHYLLIS
and YOUNG SALLY *and the rest—lined up and dancing.
Their scanty costumes are made up of bits of mirrors, and
they flash and sparkle as they move.*

*We watch as the memories upstage move in mirror-
image to the "Chorus Girls" down front. The tempo
and excitement rise, the steps and turns grow harder,
faster. Then the explosion comes as past and present
mingle: the memories join the present downstage;*
STELLA, *mirrored by* YOUNG STELLA, *light and slim, comes
dancing on: the two tunes mesh and all the girls sing
out and dance at once*)

STELLA DEEMS	GIRLS
Who's that woman? I mean I've seen That woman who's joking But choking back tears. All those glittering years. She thought that	Mirror, mirror, on the wall, Who's the saddest gal in town? Who's been riding for a fall?
Love was a matter of "Hi, there!" "Kiss me!" "Bye, there!" Who's that woman, That cheery, weary woman Who's dressing for yet one more spree? The vision's getting blurred. Isn't that absurd?	Love was a matter of "Hi, there!" "Kiss me!" "Bye, there!" Mirror, mirror, answer me. Who is she who plays the clown?
Lord, Lord, Lord! Lord, Lord, Lord, Lord, Lord! That woman is me. That woman is me, That woman is me!	Lord, Lord, Lord! Mirror, mirror! Mirror, mirror! Mirror, mirror!

(*The number ends, the memories disappear, and we are left with seven breathless middle-aged ladies. Upstage,* WEISMANN *appears*)

WEISMANN (*Calls out*) Are there any hungry actors in the house?

(WAITERS *enter upstage with an enormous banquet table piled with food. From all over, guests appear and surge up toward the table. Downstage, no one remains but* STELLA *and, in shadows, their backs to us,* PHYLLIS *and* SALLY)

STELLA DEEMS Wasn't that a blast? I love life, you know that? I've got my troubles and I take my lumps, we've got no kids, we never made much money, and a lot of folks I love are dead, but on the whole and everything considered . . . *(She loses the thread)* Where was I? *(Grinning)* What the hell, I talk too much.

(She turns and hurries to MAX, *up by the banquet table)*

CHRISTINE DONOVAN *(To* PHYLLIS, *moving downstage from the table)* I thought you were just marvelous. (PHYLLIS *looks at her blankly)* You're Phyllis aren't you? I'm Christine. I had the dressing table next to yours. *(No reaction from* PHYLLIS) Don't you remember me at all?

PHYLLIS You never liked me.

CHRISTINE DONOVAN What a thing to say.

PHYLLIS I never liked you, either. *(Looking about)* Where's a drink?

BEN *(Handing her his as he emerges from the shadows)* My pleasure.

BUDDY *(Rushing on, giving* SALLY *a hug)* Kid, you were terrific.

SALLY Did you see me?

BUDDY You were fabulous. I kept on thinking of the first time when I saw you in the show. Jeez, you were something.

(Only the STONES *and* PLUMMERS *are downstage now. Although the two couples are literally together on the stage, they are in different places in the Weismann theater; each couple neither sees nor hears the other. First one speaks, and then the other, as the scene flows freely back and forth)*

PHYLLIS Was I ravishing? You haven't said.

BEN You were delightful. How on earth did you remember it?

PHYLLIS I've no idea. Unless it's muscle memory. It's curious, the things our bodies won't forget.

SALLY Oh, Buddy, I just feel so good.

BUDDY It's been some party. I'm half-pissed. How's Ben?

SALLY I don't think Phyllis makes him happy. I see sadness in his eyes.

BUDDY I'll bet you do.

SALLY What's that supposed to mean?

BUDDY (*Swallowing his anger*) Look, Sally, I've been thinking. I'm away too much and what I thought was, nuts to all this traveling. I'll just tell them at the office that I'm finished on the road. We could go out more, have some fun. I mean, I kind of let you down sometimes, I know I do, but I'll try harder. Honestly I will. Come on, kid, let's go home.

SALLY I wouldn't leave here for the world.
(PHYLLIS *kisses* BEN. *He is startled by the gesture and his reaction is polite and unresponsive*)

PHYLLIS (*As they separate*) Gee, honey, that was swell.

BEN You took me by surprise.

PHYLLIS I love surprises. Let's hold hands and see what happens.

BUDDY We had a good life once, kid.

SALLY When?

BUDDY Don't talk like that. When we were in Seattle and the boys were young and we'd go off for weekends, all of us. Out in the country, God, how green it was, and you were laughing, like a bubble.

SALLY That was twenty years ago.

BUDDY We had it once, though. That's the point.

PHYLLIS Ben?

BEN Not now. I'm tired, Phyllis.

PHYLLIS That's right; turn off. My God, we haven't had an honest talk since '41. You think the Japs'll win the war?

BEN I'm in no mood for honest talks.

PHYLLIS I am.

BUDDY What do you want from me? It doesn't matter what I do. It's never good enough. I come home feeling great and touch you and you look at me like I've been living in some sewer.

SALLY Haven't you? You've always got a woman someplace. Oh, I know. You leave things in your pockets so I'll know.

BUDDY She lives in Dallas and her name is—

SALLY I don't want to hear it.

BUDDY Margie! Margie, that's her name. She works at Neiman's and she's got a little house. It's quiet there. She gives me books to read each time, and when I'm there we talk for hours. And she cooks for me and sews my buttons on, and when we go to bed, it's like she thought I was some kind of miracle. She's twenty-nine and pretty and

53

you know what my luck is? (SALLY *has had enough, and
starts to go*) My luck is I love you.
   (He turns and strides away)

PHYLLIS   When did you love me last? Was it ten years ago
or never? Do you ever contemplate divorce? Or suicide?
Why don't you play around? Or do you? Have you cried
much lately? Are you ever savaged by regret? Does one
day more with me seem insupportable? Or are you dead?

BEN   I have my moments.

PHYLLIS   Tell me one.

BEN   I used to wish that life were work and sleep and nothing else, that I could go from bed to desk to bed again; and
now I look at what I do and find it meaningless.

PHYLLIS   You cleft my heart.

BEN   I cleave it. Cleft is past.

PHYLLIS   Damn right. You don't much cleave it any more.
The way I wanted you. I'd come home with my panties
wringing wet. You're shocked. Why? Is my language getting bad? It used to be, before you taught me everything
I know. What was I? Just some chorus girl who lost it in
a rumble seat. Don't you remember? You were there. Son
of a bitch, I'm going to cry.
   (She bites her lip. There are no tears)

BEN   You wore a gray dress and the zipper stuck and all you
did was sob about your mother and how she'd feel if she
knew. You were terrific. See that waitress over there? I've
been wanting to make her all night.

PHYLLIS   Hallelujah, I'll be rooting for you. I wish you'd
ravage her and love it. Ben, I don't want to be old.

BEN Who does, for God's sake?

PHYLLIS Me. I did. I used to count the days. I couldn't wait till we were old enough so nothing mattered any more. I've still got time for something in my life. I want another chance. I'm still young and I'm talking to the walls. Where are you?

BEN Right where you are, and it's yes to all your questions. Yes, I loved you once and, yes, I play around and, yes, I have regrets and God, yes, one more day with you—
(He breaks off sharply, turns and strides away)

PHYLLIS *(Reaching for a drink from a passing* WAITER*)* I'll take that. You have a nice face. I don't suppose you play the drums.
(She moves to the wings. The WAITER, KEVIN, *follows. As they go,* CARLOTTA CAMPION *appears, surrounded by a small group of admiring gentlemen. They have been drinking, and there is a sense of warmth and friendliness.)*

CARLOTTA *(Quieting them down)* I had a Follies number once, a solo, and they cut the goddamn thing in Philadelphia. See, they thought it was a sad song and it kept on getting laughs. The told me sing it sadder, so I did. I got out there and gave 'em sad, and eighteen hundred people fell apart. *(She laughs at herself and shrugs)* Whatcha gonna do?
(She sings)
Good times and bum times,
I've seen them all and, my dear,
I'm still here.
Plush velvet sometimes,
Sometimes just pretzels and beer,
But I'm here.
I've stuffed the dailies

In my shoes,
Strummed ukuleles,
Sung the blues,
Seen all my dreams disappear,
But I'm here.
I've slept in shanties,
Guest of the W.P.A.,
But I'm here.
Danced in my scanties,
Three bucks a night was the pay,
But I'm here.
I've stood on bread lines
With the best,
Watched while the headlines
Did the rest.
In the Depression was I depressed?
Nowhere near.
I met a big financier
And I'm here.

I've been through Gandhi,
Windsor and Wally's affair,
And I'm here.
Amos 'n' Andy,
Mahjongg and platinum hair,
And I'm here.

I got through Abie's
Irish Rose,
Five Dionne babies,
Major Bowes,
Had heebie-jeebies
For Beebe's
Bathysphere.

I've lived through Brenda Frazier
And I'm here.

I've gotten through Herbert and J. Edgar Hoover,
Gee, that was fun and a half.
When you've been through Herbert and J. Edgar
Hoover,
Anything else is a laugh.

I've been through Reno,
I've been through Beverly Hills,
And I'm here.
Reefers and vino,
Rest cures, religion and pills,
But I'm here.
Been called a pinko
Commie tool,
Got through it stinko
By my pool.
I should have gone to an acting school,
That seems clear.
Still, someone said, "She's sincere,"
So I'm here.

Black sable one day,
Next day it goes into hock,
But I'm here.
Top billing Monday,
Tuesday you're touring in stock,
But I'm here.

First you're another
Sloe-eyed vamp,
Then someone's mother,
Then you're camp.
Then you career

From career to career.
I'm almost through my memoirs,
And I'm here.

I've gotten through "Hey, lady, aren't you whoozis?
Wow, what a looker you were."
Or, better yet, "Sorry, I thought you were whoozis,
Whatever happened to her?"

Good times and bum times,
I've seen them all and, my dear,
I'm still here.
Plush velvet sometimes,
Sometimes just pretzels and beer,
But I'm here.
I've run the gamut,
A to Z.
Three cheers and dammit,
C'est la vie.
I got through all of last year,
And I'm here.
Lord knows, at least I've been there,
And I'm here!
Look who's here!
I'm still here!

> *(The number ends in a blackout. When the lights rise, we find* BEN *and* SALLY *sitting close together in a private place. There is no one else in sight.* BEN *is looking into space)*

BEN *(His voice is quiet)* The one impulsive thing I ever did was marry Phyllis. I must have loved her very much. And these days, when I look at her, the cool I see in those blue eyes. She is untouchable. Why does she stay with me, for God's sake? She despises me, you know.

SALLY She can't; no woman could.

BEN One time, we were vacationing in Salzburg, just the two of us alone . . . *(He can't get it out)* It's a boring story.

SALLY You don't like to feel things; that's your trouble. When I have a feeling, I enjoy it. I just close my eyes and let it come. Come on, close your eyes. *(He closes his eyes)* You feeling anything?

BEN Not much.
    (We see YOUNG BEN *and* YOUNG SALLY. *She wears a slip, he trousers and T-shirt. Both are barefoot. They sit, arms tenderly around each other.* BEN *glances at his memory and quickly looks away)*

SALLY I read a lot—just trashy stuff to pass the time—and the amount of junk about love people write . . . When I loved you and you loved me . . . I float off sometimes . . . Ben, it's all I think about.

> YOUNG SALLY
> The way I'm always laughing, you'd think I was a happy girl, but I'm only happy, Ben, when I'm with you.

BEN *(Here and throughout, watching the memory)* I made love to a girl this afternoon. I do that now and then; it happens. Plain girl, no conquest there to brag about. And after it was over, guess what? I began to cry. Now, I haven't cried since childhood, and the noises that I heard come out of me . . . I would give—what have I got?—my soul's of little value, but I'd give it to be twenty-five again.

SALLY It's not too late, it never is.

BEN I've done it wrong. This isn't what I meant.

SALLY I knew it, Ben. I'm very sensitive to people's looks, and when you looked at me tonight . . .

> YOUNG SALLY
> I've got no friends. You're the only one. I couldn't live without you, Ben, I'd kill myself.

BEN I don't know who I am.

SALLY You're my sweet boy, my little Ben. I don't mind giving up the stage, and Buddy doesn't love me, not like you do. I can wait until the war is over.

> YOUNG SALLY
> I'd like to disappear inside you, just curl up and disappear.

BEN *(To his memory)* Did I love you, Sally? Was it real? *(The intensity of* BEN's *anguish is such that* YOUNG SALLY *is wrenched around by it. She looks at* BEN *and rises and moves to him lovingly, speaking as* SALLY *speaks)*

SALLY and YOUNG SALLY I'll write you letters and I'll knit you socks. I'll go half-crazy from the waiting but I'll stand it somehow. I can wait forever just so long as at the end of it there's you.

> *(*BEN *opens his arms.* YOUNG SALLY *slips into them. He sings the song and plays the scene to her.* SALLY, *too, although she stands alone, is in* BEN's *arms. She moves precisely as* YOUNG SALLY *does, as if the two of them were one)*

"Loveland"

BEN

Too many mornings,
Waking and pretending I reach for you.
Thousands of mornings,
Dreaming of my girl . . .

All that time wasted,
Merely passing through,
Time I could have spent
So content
Wasting time with you.

Too many mornings,
Wishing that the room might be filled with you,
Morning to morning,
Turning into days.
All the days
That I thought would never end,
All the nights
With another day to spend,
All those times
I'd look up to see
Sally standing at the door,
Sally moving to the bed,
Sally resting in my arms
With her head against my head.

SALLY   If you don't kiss me, Ben, I think I'm going to die.
          (*As if he were playing the scene with her, not the
          memory, she sings*)
          How I planned:
          What I'd wear tonight and
          When should I get here,
          How should I find you,
          Where I'd stand,

What I'd say in case you
Didn't remember,
How I'd remind you—
You remembered,
And my fears were wrong!
Was it ever real?
Did I ever love you this much?
Did we ever feel
So happy then?

BEN

It was always real . . .

SALLY

I should have worn green . . .

BEN

And I've always loved you this much . . .

SALLY

I wore green the last time . . .

BEN

We can always feel this happy . . .

SALLY

The time I was happy . . .
(The music soars joyously. They sing together)

BEN and SALLY

Too many mornings
Wasted in pretending I reach for you.
How many mornings
Are there still to come?

How much time can we hope that there will be?
Not much time, but it's time enough for me,
If there's time to look up and see

Sally standing at the door,
Sally moving to the bed,
Sally resting in my arms,
With your head against my head.

(As the music, soft and sweet, floats to its end, YOUNG
SALLY *drifts away, and* SALLY *slips into* BEN's *arms. They
kiss each other passionately as* YOUNG BEN *and* YOUNG
SALLY, *hand in hand, stroll off.*

As they kiss, BUDDY *appears on a platform high above
them. He is pacing, restless, close to rage. He cannot literally see his wife and* BEN *below, and the lines that oc-
casionally burst from him are directed at the walls)*

BEN *(As he and* SALLY *separate)* I want you, Sally.

SALLY Silly Ben, I know you do.

BUDDY *(From above)* I ought to take her by the hair and drag
her out of here.

BEN The way you make me feel . . . the way I need
you . . .

SALLY Don't you always?

BEN Let's get out of here.

BUDDY I could of been somebody but no guts. I had no
guts.

SALLY *(Holding back as he takes her hand to go)* Just one
thing, Ben.

BEN Come on.

SALLY We're getting married, aren't we?
(BEN stops, frozen, looks at her as YOUNG BEN *and* YOUNG
SALLY *reappear. He wears a sailor suit. She wears a coat.
They are walking down a street)*

BUDDY   What do I see in her, for God's sake?

SALLY   I mean, this time you're going to marry me. Aren't you?

> YOUNG SALLY
> You love me, Ben.

SALLY   You love me, Ben. That's what people do when they're in love. They get married.

> YOUNG SALLY
> Why not get married now?

BEN   *(His attention torn between the present and the past)*   Oh my God, what am I doing?

> YOUNG BEN
> There's lots of time for that.

SALLY   Sally wants another kiss, please.

> YOUNG SALLY
> What if there's not?

BEN   I must be insane.

SALLY   We'll be so happy, we'll be—

> YOUNG SALLY
> What if you don't come back?

> YOUNG BEN
> Don't worry, lawyers don't
> get shot.

> YOUNG SALLY
> What if there's someone else?
> Ben, marry me.

BEN   Sally, listen.

SALLY   I'll make you the best wife.

YOUNG BEN
Sure, sure.

YOUNG SALLY
Now. If you really love me.

YOUNG BEN *(Irritation rising)*
Love you, yes, I love you.

YOUNG SALLY
Then why not?

BEN   Listen to me, Sally!

SALLY   Sure, Ben; every word.

BEN   I'm not myself.

YOUNG BEN
I'm late.

BEN   It's this damn place, all the drink.

YOUNG SALLY
Ben Stone!

SALLY   There's lipstick on your collar.

YOUNG SALLY
I want to know.

BEN   Where? That's all I need, where is it?

YOUNG BEN
Quit pressing me.

SALLY   April Fool—I get you every time.

YOUNG SALLY
I want a reason, damn it.
(YOUNG BEN *strides off.* YOUNG
SALLY *stands glaring after him*)

BEN I'm sorry—all the things I've done and didn't do—but,
Sally, all of it was over years ago.
     (Distraught, BEN *turns, half-stumbles offstage.* SALLY *speaks
     as if he were still there. Her voice is sweet and even)*

SALLY I know it was. I'm all right, Ben. Don't get upset.
It's fine. We're going to be just fine.
     (As SALLY *finishes her line she is standing next to* YOUNG
     SALLY, *and they exit side by side, as if reality and memory
     had come together. As they go off,* BUDDY *bursts into
     angry song)*

BUDDY
          The right girl—yeah!
          The right girl,
          She makes you feel like a million bucks
          Instead of—what?—like a rented tux.

          The right girl—yeah!
          The right girl,
          She's with you, no matter how you feel,
          You're not the good guy, you're not the heel.
          You're not the dreamboat that sank—you're real
          When you got—yeah!
          The right girl—yeah!
          And I got—
               *(He has no words for what he's got. Instead, he bursts
               into angry dance, leaping down stairs, twisting, tapping
               without tap shoes all the fury and regret he feels. Then,
               without preparation, the music changes and the anger's
               gone and* BUDDY *sings)*
          Hey, Margie, I'm back, babe.
          Come help me unpack, babe.
          Hey, Margie, hey, bright girl,
          I'm home.

What's new, babe? You miss me?
You smell good, come kiss me.
Hey, Margie, you wanna go dancing?
I'm home.

Des Moines was rotten and the deal fell through.
I pushed, babe.
I'm bushed, babe.
I needed you to tell my troubles to—
The heck, babe—
Let's neck, babe.
Hey, Margie,
You wanna go dancing?
You wanna go driving? or something?
Okay, babe,
Whatever you say, babe—
You wanna stay home!
You wanna stay home!
   *(He holds an imagined Margie in his arms and dances
   with her tenderly; then)*
Hey Margie, it's day, babe,
My flight goes—No, stay, babe,
You know how you cry, babe—
Stay home.

Be good now, we'll speak, babe,
It might be next week, babe—
Hey, Margie—goodbye, babe—
I gotta go home.
   (The angry music of the opening returns)
The right girl—yeah!
The right girl,
She sees you're nothing and thinks you're king,
She knows you got other songs to sing.
You still could be—hell, well anything

When you got—yeah!
The right girl—
And I got . . .

(The dance is more than angry now; it's desperate as
BUDDY *hurls himself about the stage at non-existent barri-*
ers. The dance ends. He begins to speak, as if rehearsing.
His voice is oddly quiet)

Sally, I want to talk. See, I've been thinking, oh, all kinds
of thoughts, like how it is at home with you. The mess,
the moods, the spells you get, in bed for days without a
word. Or else you're crying, God the tears around our
place—or flying out to Tom and Tim and camping on
their doorstep just to fight—

*(*SALLY *appears above him, high up on a flight of stairs.*
She stops and listens)

—it's crazy and we're finished, kid; that's all she wrote.
It's over.

SALLY Don't feel bad, darling. You'll be better off without
me, and I'm going to be just fine. You see, Ben wants to
marry me. He asked me if I'd marry him and naturally
I said I would.

BUDDY Is that a fact.

SALLY *(Nodding)* He's home now packing, and we're leav-
ing in the morning.

BUDDY Take you to a hotel, sure; but marry you? You're
either drunk or crazy and I don't care which.

SALLY He held me and the band was playing. I can even
tell you what the tune was.

BUDDY *(In a rage)* I've spent my whole life making things
the way you want them, and no matter what we do or
where we go or what we've got, it isn't what you want.

It used to drive me nuts. Not any more. So you wake up hung over or you wake up in the funny farm, it's all the goddamn same to me.

(He wheels, strides off)

SALLY He took me in his arms and kissed me. I know every word he said. I'm getting married and I'm going to live forever with the man I love. Oh dear Lord, isn't it a wonder?

(She sits quietly, smiling, arms tight around herself. In a downstage corner, lights find BEN and CARLOTTA CAMPION. She is laughing, soft and throaty. He sits near her, tense and, at the same time, fairly drunk)

BEN Just meet me later. I don't want to be alone, that's all.

CARLOTTA *(Warm, wry, boozy)* You're married; you can play around. I'm in-between; I never cheat on guys I'm living with.

BEN I only want to talk. I've got to talk to somebody. Just be with me.

CARLOTTA *(Patting him)* Come on, come on now; you're a big boy.

BEN *(He looks up, smiles lopsidedly)* Right you are. I'll tell you fascinating tales of my adventures, make you laugh.

CARLOTTA It's nothing, you'll feel better in the morning.

BEN Take me home and hold me. Jesus, please.

CARLOTTA We had some fun once; it was just a thing. That's all you meant to me, Ben: just a thing. *(She cradles his head in her lap and gently touches his hair)* The guy I'm living with, he's just a thing, too, but he's twenty-six. I like him. I liked you. Next year, I'll like some other guy. Men are so sweet.

(A spotlight picks out HEIDI SCHILLER *in the darkness high upstage. She is sitting, isolated, head tilted back, eyes closed in reverie. Her voice, as she begins to sing, is high, silvery, crystalline. Midway,* YOUNG HEIDI *appears, and the song becomes a duet, an old voice and a young one, twined about each other)*

HEIDI

    One more kiss before we part,
    One more kiss and—farewell,
    Never shall we meet again,
    Just a kiss and then
    We break the spell.

    One more kiss to melt the heart,
    One more glimpse of the past,

HEIDI and YOUNG HEIDI

    One more souvenir of bliss
    Knowing well that this
    One must be the last.

    Dreams are a sweet mistake.
    All dreamers must awake.

                    YOUNG HEIDI
                    On, then, with the
                    dance,
                    No backward glance
                    Or my heart will break.
                    Never look back.

HEIDI

    Never look back.
    One more kiss before we part.

                    YOUNG HEIDI
                    Not with tears or a sigh.

HEIDI and YOUNG HEIDI
All things beautiful must die.

YOUNG HEIDI
Now that our love is
done,

HEIDI
Lover, give me . . .

HEIDI and YOUNG HEIDI
. . . One
More kiss and—goodbye.
(*The lights fade from* HEIDI *and* YOUNG HEIDI, *come up
dimly in another area. We see a couple necking. It is*
PHYLLIS *and* KEVIN, *the* WAITER *she spoke to earlier. He
nuzzles her as she speaks*)

PHYLLIS   I used to wish I had a son. *(She looks straight ahead
at nothing)* I was going to call him Eddie, and I used to
go to shops to look for things for him to wear. I'd see a
nightshirt on the counter, pick it up and hold it in my
hands—Young man, you're getting me all wet.

KEVIN   Now, that's a hell of a remark.

PHYLLIS   I don't know what we're doing here.

KEVIN   *(Feelings hurt)*   This wasn't my idea. You started it.

PHYLLIS   All right, all right; you've been assaulted by a crazy
lady. Where's a drink?

KEVIN   I'll get my tray.

PHYLLIS   Come here. *(He hesitates)* The moon's gone down;
you're safe. *(As he brings her a drink)* Now that we've been
introduced, tell me: do you find me attractive?

KEVIN   I dunno—Yeah, I do. It beats me.

PHYLLIS   Thanks. Do you sleep around a lot?

KEVIN   Sure, all the time.

PHYLLIS   Same girl or different?

KEVIN   Different.

PHYLLIS   Do you find, in your experience, does that make sex less pleasurable?

KEVIN   Does what?

PHYLLIS   Not loving anyone.

KEVIN   Hell, I dunno. I never think about it.

PHYLLIS   *(Her face starts to fall apart)* That's a neat trick.

KEVIN   Hey, what's the matter?

PHYLLIS   If I knew, I'd have it fixed. *(She turns away, moves thoughtfully to* BEN, *who sits slumped in a corner, half asleep.* KEVIN *drifts away)* Ben, do you know, according to statistics, that I can't expect to die till 1995? That's one long time, and I've been considering what my options are. Hell, even on the gallows, there are choices: you can take it like a man or cry a lot. What's there for me? I can't go home to mother; she's dead. No, Ben, it all comes down to this: I won't go back to what we've had, not one day more of it.

BEN   *(Slowly raising his head)* I've got it all worked out. The walls are closing in but there's a door. And, lady, it's for you. I don't know how I've stood it all these years. The only thing I want from you is a divorce.

PHYLLIS   Get him: puppy love at fifty-three. I see you both in your bikinis, honeymooning at St. Petersburg. She'll make a hit at the foundation in her tap shoes.

BEN I'm not in love with Sally. Hell, I never was. There's no one in my life; there's nothing. That's what's killing me.

PHYLLIS I'm nothing. That's not much.

BEN God, I see lovers on the streets—it's real, it's going on out there and I can't reach it. Someone's got to love me and I don't care if it doesn't last a month, I don't care if I'm ludicrous or who she is or what she looks like, I don't care.

PHYLLIS You haven't got a clue what love is. Hell, you've had it all your life. I should have left you years ago.

BEN Just leave me now, that's all I want.

PHYLLIS I thought you needed me.

BEN For what? To tell me I'm a fake? I don't need you for that. I know it. Doesn't everybody? Jesus, can't they see it? Are they blind? They look at me and I keep waiting for them all to point and say, "You! Stone! I know what you are."

PHYLLIS (*Seated, soft and very still, as if thinking aloud. She hasn't heard a word since she spoke last*)
Leave you? Leave you?
How could I leave you?
How could I go it alone?
Could I wave the years away
With a quick goodbye?
How do you wipe tears away
When your eyes are dry?
Sweetheart, lover,
Could I recover,
Give up the joys I have known?
Not to fetch your pills again

Every day at five,
Not to give those dinners for ten
Elderly men
From the U.N.—
How could I survive?

Could I leave you
And your shelves of the World's Best Books
And the evenings of martyred looks,
Cryptic sighs,
Sullen glares from those injured eyes?
Leave the quips with a sting, jokes with a sneer,
Passionless love-making once a year?
Leave the lies ill-concealed
And the wounds never healed
And the games not worth winning
And—wait, I'm just beginning!
What, leave you, leave you,
How could I leave you?
What would I do on my own?
Putting thoughts of you aside
In the South of France,
Would I think of suicide?
Darling, shall we dance?

Could I live through the pain
On a terrace in Spain?
Would it pass? It would pass.
Could I bury my rage
With a boy half your age
In the grass? Bet your ass.
But I've done that already—or didn't you know, love?
Tell me, how could I leave when I left long ago, love?

Could I leave you?
No, the point is, could you leave me?

Well, I guess you could leave me the house,
Leave me the flat,
Leave me the Braques and Chagalls and all that.
You could leave me the stocks for sentiment's sake
And ninety percent of the money you make,
And the rugs
And the cooks—
Darling, you keep the drugs,
Angel, you keep the books,
Honey, I'll take the grand,
Sugar, you keep the spinet
And all of our friends and—
Just wait a goddam minute!
Oh,
Leave you? Leave you?
How could I leave you?
Sweetheart, I have to confess:
Could I leave you?
Yes.
Will I leave you?
Will *I* leave *You?*
Guess!

    *(Her eyes bore in at him. The stage is empty and the
light is strange)*

BEN *(Looking at his hands)* They won't stop shaking.
    (As he jams them into his pockets, YOUNG BEN *appears
upstage and says to an enraptured* YOUNG PHYLLIS)

                    YOUNG BEN
             You'll make a good wife,
             Phyl.

                    YOUNG PHYLLIS
             I'll try. Oh, Ben, I'll try so
             hard. I'll study and I'll read—

I'm not much now, I know
that—and I'll walk my feet off
in the Metropolitan Museum.

PHYLLIS   I tried so hard. I studied and I read—I thought I
wasn't much: I was terrific—and I walked my goddamn
feet off. (*Turning to* YOUNG PHYLLIS) What happened to
you, Phyl?

YOUNG PHYLLIS
I love you, Ben.

BEN (*To* YOUNG BEN)   She did—and what did you give her?

YOUNG BEN
Someday, I'll have the biggest
goddamn limousine.

BEN (*To* YOUNG BEN, *with loathing*)   You were so smart.

PHYLLIS (*To* YOUNG PHYLLIS)   Where did you go?

YOUNG PHYLLIS
We've got each other, Ben.
What difference does it make?

BEN (*To* YOUNG BEN)   You had it all and you threw it away.

BUDDY (*Steaming on stage*)   There you are, you bastard.

BEN (*The memory figures stay in place as* BEN *wrenches himself
into the present*)   What's that?

BUDDY   You're a fourteen-carat bastard.

YOUNG   BUDDY   (*Appearing,
moving to* YOUNG BEN)
You're my best friend, best I
ever had, Ben.

BEN *(To* BUDDY) What's all this about?

YOUNG BUDDY *(To* YOUNG BEN) You wouldn't screw around with Sally. Take her dancing, maybe, but that's all, right?

YOUNG BEN *(To* YOUNG BUDDY) She's a sweet kid but that's where it stops.

BUDDY and YOUNG BUDDY *(To* BEN *and* YOUNG BEN *respectively)* I'll knock your goddamn block off.

BEN and YOUNG BEN Any time you say.

SALLY *(Coming on in dreamland with* YOUNG SALLY, *smiling sweetly as she moves to* BEN) I'm ready, darling. We can go now.

PHYLLIS *(To* BEN) You're not in love with Sally. Boy, you take the cake.

SALLY *(To* BEN) Let's go to my place. Phyl won't be there.

BEN But I never said I loved you, did I?

YOUNG SALLY *(To* YOUNG BEN) Now, if you really love me.

YOUNG BEN *(To* YOUNG SALLY) Love you, yes, I love you.

YOUNG SALLY
Then why not?

YOUNG BUDDY *(To* YOUNG SALLY) You really love me, don't you, kid?
(Turning to him)

YOUNG SALLY
With all my heart, oh Buddy
. . .

BUDDY (*To* YOUNG SALLY) That's a lie.

SALLY (*To* BEN) Please, Ben, I'd like to go now.

BUDDY (*To* SALLY) Ben ran out and I was there: that's all it was.

YOUNG SALLY (*To* YOUNG BEN) I want a reason. Am I cheap? Is that it? I'm not good enough.

YOUNG BEN (*To* YOUNG SALLY) Think what you goddamn please.

YOUNG SALLY
Don't leave me, Ben. I'll kill myself, I'll die!

SALLY (*Turning on* YOUNG SALLY) You fool!

PHYLLIS (*To* BEN) I want a baby, Ben.

SALLY (*To* YOUNG SALLY) You could of had him but you played it wrong.

YOUNG PHYLLIS (*To* YOUNG BEN) Ben, can't we have one, can't we try?

SIMULTANEOUSLY

SALLY (*To* YOUNG SALLY) You had him crazy for you but let him up your skirts too soon!

BUDDY (*To* YOUNG BUDDY) You took her back. She two-timed you and you married her.

78

SIMULTANEOUSLY

PHYLLIS (*To* BEN) I see you now, right through you. Hollow, that's what you are. You're an empty place.

BEN (*To* YOUNG BEN) You never loved her, why'd you marry her? Because it made sense? Is that all, for Christ's sake?

NOW ALL FOUR SIMULTANEOUSLY
(Each of them turns on his past self. With mounting rage, as if they meant to do physical violence to the memories)

BEN (*To* YOUNG BEN) Smart. You knew what you were doing: both eyes open. You can't spend your life with someone you don't love. It's crazy. You unfeeling bastard, on the make. Look what you've done to me!

BUDDY (*To* YOUNG BUDDY) She never loved you and you knew it. In your guts you damn well knew it. What did you expect, for Chrissake, married to a girl like that. You pissed my life away, that's what you did to me.

PHYLLIS (*To* YOUNG PHYLLIS) He never loved you and you knew it. Deep down in your guts, you knew. You thought he'd change. If you loved him enough. You silly bitch, you fool, you threw my life away!

SALLY (*To* YOUNG SALLY) The only man I ever wanted, and you lost him for me. Everything, you lost me everything. You tramp. You left me here with nothing. I could kill you. I could die!

NOW ALL EIGHT SIMULTANEOUSLY
(It's senseless now, completely unintelligible and rather frightening)

YOUNG BUDDY (*To* YOUNG SALLY) Baby, I love you so much. The moon, I'll buy it for you. Everything you ever wanted, baby, that's what Buddy's gonna get for you.	YOUNG SALLY (*To* YOUNG BUDDY) Honey, you're the only one. The things you do to me, the way you make me feel. I love it, Buddy. Jeez, I love you.	YOUNG PHYLLIS (*To* YOUNG BEN) Dearest, oh my dearest Ben, I'll be so good for you, you'll be so happy. I'll be everything you ever wanted, just for you.	YOUNG BEN (*To* YOUNG PHYLLIS) Darling, to the top. That's where we're going: straight up. And the view from there, the view is something.
BUDDY (*To* YOUNG BUDDY) I could of had a great life all along. I had the wrong wife, that was all. You've screwed me and I'll get you for it!	SALLY (*To* YOUNG SALLY) I'll pay you back, that's what I'll do. For all the things I never had. You're gonna pay!	PHYLLIS (*To* YOUNG PHYLLIS) I've had no life, I haven't lived. You can't do what you've done to me and get away with it!	BEN (*To* YOUNG BEN) You killed me. I've been dead for thirty years. It's all your work. You did it!

(As the madness of the confrontation hits its peak—just as there seems to be no possible way out—drums start to roll, trumpeters in Medieval costumes emerge from the shadows, heavenly music is heard, drop after drop comes flying down, all valentines and lace, and as the lights rise to bright gold, dancers, young and beautiful, all dressed like DRESDEN DOLLS *and* CAVALIERS, *appear.* BEN, PHYLLIS, BUDDY *and* SALLY, *eyes wild, and half-demented, stand in the midst of it all, taking their first look at "Loveland")*

CHORUS

Time stops, hearts are young,
Only serenades are sung
In Loveland,
Where everybody lives to love.

Raindrops never rain,
Every road is lovers' lane
In Loveland,
Where everybody loves to live.

See that sunny sun and honeymoon,
There where seven hundred days hath June.

Sweetheart, take my hand,
Let us find that wondrous land
Called Loveland, Loveland, Loveland . . .

FIRST CAVALIER *(As he speaks, in an archway for upstage a vision of delight appears: a towering, ravishing* SHOWGIRL *in extraordinary costume. Her costume, like the ones that follow, has a theme. This time it's "music," and her vast hoop skirt is encrusted with lutes and harps, entwined with strands of pearls and swags of silk and God-knows-what. Above the skirt, a long expanse of naked midriff, a modest bodice and, on top, a soaring headdress.)*

To lovers' ears, a lover's voice is music,

A song that no one but a lover knows.
*(As he speaks, she makes her majestic way downstage,
parading for us all to see.* BEN, PHYLLIS, BUDDY *and* SALLY
stand at the sides now, watching)

CHORUS
Loveland, where everybody lives to love.

SECOND CAVALIER *(Speaking)*
To lovers' lips, a lover's lips are petals,
A velvet promise budding like a rose.
(And a second SHOWGIRL, *hoop skirt garlanded with blos-
soms, joins the first)*

CHORUS
Loveland, where everybody loves to live.

THIRD CAVALIER *(Speaking as third* SHOWGIRL *enters)*
The lover is transported by his rapture,
As ever heavenwards his heart ascends.

CHORUS
Loveland, Loveland . . .

FOURTH CAVALIER *(Speaking as a fourth* SHOWGIRL *enters)*
The lover's heart contains a lover's secret,
Which only the beloved comprehends.

CHORUS
Loveland, Loveland . . .

FIFTH CAVALIER *(Speaking as a fifth* SHOWGIRL *enters)*
Two lovers are like lovebirds in devotion,
If separated, they must swoon and die.

CHORUS
Loveland, where everybody lives to love.

SIXTH CAVALIER *(Speaking as a sixth* SHOWGIRL *enters)*
>To lovers' eyes, a lover's eyes are jewels,
>More radiant than the stars that light the sky.

CHORUS
>Loveland, where everybody loves to live.

>Lovers pine and sigh but never part,
>Time is measured by a beating heart.

>Bells ring, fountains splash,
>Folks use kisses 'stead of cash
>In Loveland, Loveland . . .

>Love, Love, Loveland . . .
>Love, Love, Loveland . . .
>Love!
>>*(As "Loveland" ends, the stage is full of* DRESDEN DOLLS *and* CAVALIERS *and* SHOWGIRLS. *They strike a decorative pose and hold it as new music, bright and rhythmic now, begins.*
>>YOUNG BEN *and* YOUNG PHYLLIS *come dancing on downstage. Memories no more, they sport bright colors and pink cheeks. They flash adoring smiles at one another and begin to sing)*

YOUNG BEN
>What will tomorrow bring?
>The pundits query.

YOUNG PHYLLIS
>Will it be cheery?

YOUNG BEN
>Will it be sad?

YOUNG PHYLLIS
>Will it be birds in spring
>Or hara-kiri?

YOUNG BEN

Don't worry, dearie.

YOUNG PHYLLIS

Don't worry, lad.

YOUNG BEN

I'll have our future suit your whim,
Blue chip preferred.

YOUNG PHYLLIS

Putting it in a synonym,
Perfect's the word.

YOUNG BEN and **YOUNG PHYLLIS**

(BEN *and* PHYLLIS, *almost as if against their will, are
drawn forward and stand close to their young selves,
watching, listening to what was or never was or might
have been*)
We're in this thing together,
Aren'tcha glad?
Each day from now will be
The best day you ever had.

YOUNG BEN

You're gonna love tomorrow.

YOUNG PHYLLIS

Mm-hm.

YOUNG BEN

You're gonna be with me.

YOUNG PHYLLIS

Mm-hm.

YOUNG BEN

You're gonna love tomorrow,
I'm giving you my personal guarantee.

YOUNG PHYLLIS
> Say toodle-oo to sorrow.

YOUNG BEN
> Mm-hm.

YOUNG PHYLLIS
> And fare-thee-well, ennui.

YOUNG BEN
> Bye-bye.

YOUNG PHYLLIS
> You're gonna love tomorrow
> As long as your tomorrow is spent with me.

YOUNG BEN and YOUNG PHYLLIS
> Today was perfectly perfect,
> You say.
> Well, don't go away,
> 'Cause if you think you liked today,
>
> You're gonna *love* tomorrow.
> Mm-hm.
> You stick around and see.
> Mm-hm.
> And if you love tomorrow,
> Then think of how it's gonna be:
> Tomorrow's what you're gonna have a lifetime of
> With me!
> > (YOUNG PHYLLIS *and* YOUNG BEN *dance gaily off, drawing* BEN *and* PHYLLIS *after them. As they go,* YOUNG BUDDY *and* YOUNG SALLY *dance on, hand in hand, immediately bursting into song*)

YOUNG BUDDY
> Sally, dear,
> Now that we're

Man and wife,
I will do
Wonders to
Make your life
Soul-stirring
And free of care.

YOUNG SALLY

If we fight
(And we might),
I'll concede.
Furthermore,
Dear, should your
Ego need
Bolstering,
I'll do my share.

YOUNG BUDDY

But though I'll try my utmost to see you never frown,

YOUNG SALLY

And though I'll try to cut most of our expenses down,

YOUNG BUDDY

I've some traits, I warn you,
To which you'll have objections.

YOUNG SALLY

I, too, have a cornu-
Copia of imperfections.
(BUDDY *and* SALLY, *like* BEN *and* PHYLLIS *before them, are
drawn to their young selves. They stand and watch*)
I may burn the toast.

YOUNG BUDDY

Oh, well,
I may make a rotten host.

YOUNG SALLY
> Do tell.

YOUNG BUDDY and YOUNG SALLY
> But no matter what goes wrong,
> Love will see us through
> Till something better comes along.

YOUNG BUDDY
> I may vex your folks.

YOUNG SALLY
> Okay.
> I may interrupt your jokes.

YOUNG BUDDY
> You may.

YOUNG BUDDY and YOUNG SALLY
> But if I come on too strong,
> Love will see us through
> Till something better comes along.

YOUNG BUDDY
> I may play cards all night
> And come home at three.

YOUNG SALLY
> Just leave a light
> On the porch for me.

YOUNG BUDDY and YOUNG SALLY
> Well, nobody's perfect!

YOUNG SALLY
> I may trump your ace.

YOUNG BUDDY
> Please do.
> I may clutter up the place.

YOUNG SALLY
> Me, too.

YOUNG BUDDY and YOUNG SALLY
> But the minute we embrace
> To love's old sweet song,
> Dear, that will see us through
> Till something better comes along.
>> (YOUNG BEN *and* YOUNG PHYLLIS *dance on again, exchanging greetings as they did in "Waiting for the Girls Upstairs" with* YOUNG BUDDY *and* YOUNG SALLY. BUDDY *and* SALLY *drift quietly away, and everyone left onstage is young and beautiful*)

YOUNG SALLY   Hi.

YOUNG BEN   Girls.

YOUNG PHYLLIS   Ben.

YOUNG BUDDY   Sally. *(Dancing, smiling, much in love, they sail into a double duet)*

YOUNG SALLY	YOUNG BEN
I may burn the toast.	You're gonna love tomorrow.
YOUNG BUDDY	
Oh, well. I may make a rotten host.	YOUNG PHYLLIS
	Mm-hm.
YOUNG SALLY	
Do tell.	

YOUNG BUDDY and YOUNG
SALLY
But no matter what goes
wrong,
Love will see us through
Till something better comes
along.

YOUNG BUDDY
I may vex your folks.

YOUNG SALLY
Okay. I may interrupt your
jokes.

YOUNG BUDDY
You may.

YOUNG BUDDY and YOUNG
SALLY
But if I come on too strong,
Love will see us through
till something better comes
along.

YOUNG BUDDY
I may play cards all night
and come home at three.

YOUNG BEN
You're gonna be with me.

YOUNG PHYLLIS
Mm-hm.

YOUNG BEN
You're gonna love tomor-
row,
I'm giving you my personal
guarantee.

YOUNG PHYLLIS
Say toodle-oo to sorrow.

YOUNG BEN
Mm-hm.

YOUNG PHYLLIS
And fare-thee-well, ennui.

YOUNG BEN
Bye-bye.

YOUNG BEN and YOUNG
PHYLLIS
You're gonna love tomor-
row,
As long as your tomorrow is
spent with me.
Today was perfectly per-
fect, you say.

YOUNG SALLY
Just leave a light
on the porch for me.

YOUNG BUDDY and YOUNG
SALLY
Well, nobody's perfect!

YOUNG SALLY
I may trump your ace.

YOUNG BUDDY
Please do. I may clutter up
the place.

YOUNG SALLY
Me, too.

YOUNG BUDDY and YOUNG
SALLY
But the minute we embrace
To love's old sweet song,
Dear, that will see us
through
Till something,
Love will keep us true
Till something,
Love will help us hew
To something,
Love will have to do
Till something better comes
along!

Well, don't go away,
'cause if you think you liked
today,

You're gonna *love* tomor-
row,
Mm-hm.
You stick around and see.
Mm-hm.

YOUNG BEN and YOUNG
PHYLLIS
And if you love tomorrow,
Then think of how it's
gonna be.
Tomorrow's what you're
gonna have,
And Monday's what you're
gonna have,
And April's what you're
gonna have,
And love is what you're
gonna have
A lifetime of
With me!

*(A show curtain drops in downstage as the number
ends.* BUDDY *pops his head through the curtain, grins at
us engagingly and sings)*

BUDDY

Hello, folks, we're into the Follies!

First, though, folks, we'll pause for a mo'.

No, no, folks, you'll still get your jollies—

It's just I got a problem that I think you should know.

See, I've been very perturbed of late, very upset,

Very betwixt and between.

The things that I want, I don't seem to get.

The things that I get—You know what I mean?

(He steps through the curtain into full view. He is in his Follies costume now—plaid baggy pants, bright blue jacket and a shiny derby hat. Suspended from his waist, traveling salesman that he is, is a plywood model car big enough for him to sit and scoot around in)

I've got those

"God-why-don't-you-love-me-oh-you-do-I'll-see-you-later"

Blues,

That

"Long-as-you-ignore-me-you're-the-only-thing-that-matters"

Feeling,

That

"If-I'm-good-enough-for-you-you're-not-good-enough-And-thank-you-for-the-present-but-what's-wrong-with-it?" stuff,

Those

"Don't-come-any-closer-'cause-you-know-how-much-I-love-you"

Feelings,

Those

"Tell-me-that-you-love-me-oh-you-did-I-gotta-run-now"

Blues.

(A CHORUS GIRL *comes flouncing on, as a caricature of his beloved Margie)*
Margie, oh Margie!
She says she really loves me.

"MARGIE"   I love you.

BUDDY
—She says.
She says she really cares.

"MARGIE"   I care. I care.

BUDDY
She says that I'm her hero.

"MARGIE"   My hero.

BUDDY
—She says.
I'm perfect, she swears.

"MARGIE"   You're perfect, goddammit.

BUDDY
She says that if we parted,

"MARGIE"   If we parted.

BUDDY
—She says,
She says that she'd be sick.

"MARGIE"   Bleah.

BUDDY
She says she's mine forever—

"MARGIE"   Forever.

BUDDY
—She says.
I gotta get outta here quick!

"MARGIE" Don't go! I love you!
(BUDDY *scoots off, trying to escape from her embrace.*
"MARGIE" *pursues him. He turns his car around and
chases her to the wings*)

BUDDY
I've got those
"Whisper-how-I'm-better-than-I-think-but-what-do-
you-know?"
Blues,
That
"Why-do-you-keep-telling-me-I-stink-when-I-adore-
you"
Feeling,
That
"Say-I'm-all-the-world-to-you-you're-out-of-your-
mind-
I-know-there's-someone-else-and-I-could-kiss-your-
behind,"
Those
"You-say-I'm-terrific-but-your-taste-was-always-
rotten"
Feelings,
Those
"Go-away-I-need-you,"
"Come-to-me-I'll-kill-you,"
"Darling-I'll-do-anything-to-keep-you-with-me-till-
you-
Tell-me-that-you-love-me-oh-you-did-now-beat-it-
will-you?"
Blues.

(Another CHORUS GIRL, *this time a cartoon of Sally, hip-
swings her way onstage)*
Sally, oh Sally . . .
She says she loves another—

"SALLY"   Another.

BUDDY
   —She says,
   A fella she prefers.

"SALLY"   Furs. Furs.

BUDDY
   She says that he's her idol.

"SALLY"   Idolidolidolidol . . .

BUDDY
   —She says.
   Ideal, she avers.

"SALLY"   You deal . . . "avers"!?

BUDDY
   She says that anybody—

"SALLY"   Buddy—Bleah!

BUDDY
   —She says,
   Would suit her more than I.

"SALLY"   Aye, aye, aye.

BUDDY
   She says that I'm a washout—

"SALLY"   *(Mouthed)*   A washout!

94

BUDDY
　　—She says.
　　I love her so much, I could die!

"SALLY"　Get outta here!
　　　　(BUDDY *tears around in his car trying to catch her.* "MAR-
　　　　GIE" *returns from the wings. There is a collision involv-
　　　　ing all three of them and, when they untangle them-
　　　　selves, they sing*)

BUDDY, "MARGIE" and "SALLY"
　　I've got those
　　"God-why-don't-you-love-me-oh-you-do-I'll-see-you-
　　later"
　　Blues,
　　That
　　"Long-as-you-ignore-me-you're-the-only-thing-that-
　　matters"
　　Feeling,
　　That
　　"If-I'm-good-enough-for-you-you're-not-good-enough-
　　And-thank-you-for-the-present-but-what's-wrong-
　　with-it?" stuff,
　　Those
　　"Don't-come-any-closer-'cause-you-know-how-much-
　　I-love-you"
　　Feelings,
　　Those
　　"If-you-will-then-I-can't,"
　　"If-you-don't-then-I-gotta,"
　　"Give-it-to-me-I-don't-want-it-if-you-won't-I-gotta-
　　have-it"
　　"High-low-wrong-right-yes-no-black-white,"

"God-why-don't-you-love-me-oh-you-do-I'll-see-you-
later"
Blues.

> *(The number ends as they chase one another offstage.*
> *The lights dim down, the show curtain parts just enough*
> *to form a graceful frame, and standing there is* SALLY. *She*
> *is costumed in a clinging, beaded silver gown, as if she*
> *were a screen seductress from the 1930's. Standing very*
> *still, she sings)*

SALLY

The sun comes up,
I think about you.
The coffee cup,
I think about you.
I want you so,
It's like I'm losing my mind.

The morning ends,
I think about you.
I talk to friends,
I think about you.
And do they know?
It's like I'm losing my mind.

All afternoon,
Doing every little chore,
The thought of you stays bright.
Sometimes I stand
In the middle of the floor,
Not going left,
Not going right.

I dim the lights
And think about you,
Spend sleepless nights

To think about you.
You said you loved me,
Or were you just being kind?
Or am I losing my mind?

I want you so,
It's like I'm losing my mind.
Does no one know?
It's like I'm losing my mind.

All afternoon,
Doing every little chore,
The thought of you stays bright.
Sometimes I stand
In the middle of the floor,
Not going left,
Not going right.

I dim the lights
And think about you,
Spend sleepless nights
To think about you.
You said you loved me,
Or were you just being kind?
Or am I losing my mind?

(The lights dim. We can just see SALLY'S *face in pinpoint spotlight as the curtain gently closes. There is a jazzy blare of trumpets, the lights abruptly rise and* PHYLLIS *struts onstage wearing a short, fringe-skirted bright red dress that exposes long and shapely legs. She throws a knowing grin at us and sings)*

PHYLLIS

Here's a little story that should make you cry
About two unhappy dames.

Let us call them Lucy "X" and Jessie "Y,"
Which are not their real names.
Now Lucy has the purity
Along with the unsurety
That comes with being only twenty-one.
Jessie has maturity
And plenty of security.
Whatever you can do with them she's done.
Given their advantages,
You may ask why
The two ladies have such grief.
This is my belief,
In brief:

> *(She turns upstage, the show curtain parts. The valentines and lace of Loveland are gone, and in their place are mirrored drops of stylized archways and fountains. Reflected in the mirrors, their backs to us, are rows and rows of* CHORUS BOYS *in flaming red top hats and tails.* PHYLLIS *dances among them as she sings)*

Lucy is juicy
But terribly drab.
Jessie is dressy
But cold as a slab.
Lucy wants to be dressy,
Jessie wants to be juicy.
Lucy wants to be Jessie,
And Jessie Lucy.
You see, Jessie is racy
But hard as a rock.
Lucy is lacy
But dull as a smock.
Jessie wants to be lacy,
Lucy wants to be Jessie.

That's the sorrowful précis.
It's very messy.

Poor sad souls,
Itching to be switching roles.
Lucy wants to do what Jessie does,
Jessie wants to be what Lucy was.
Lucy's a lassie
You pat on the head.
Jessie is classy
But virtually dead.
Lucy wants to be classy,
Jessie wants to be Lassie.
If Lucy and Jessie could only combine,
I could tell you someone
Who would finally feel just fine.
   (*Everyone is dancing now. As the number builds to a cli-*
   max, we hear the CHORUS BOYS *chanting, loud and rhyth-*
   mic, through the blaring of the orchestra)

CHORUS
   Now if you see Lucy "X,"
   Youthful, truthful Lucy "X,"
   Let her know she's better than she suspects.
   Now if you see Jessie "Y,"
   Faded, jaded Jessie "Y,"
   Tell her that she's sweller than apple pie.
   Juicy Lucy,
   Dressy Jessie,
   Tell them that they ought to get together quick,
   'Cause getting it together is the whole trick.
      (*The number ends. The stage is cleared.* PHYLLIS *is the*
      last to leave. She goes, casting a look over her shoulder as
      BEN *appears. He wears dazzling white top hat and tails*

and carries a clear plastic cane. As he strikes pose after elegant pose, like a debonair man-about-town, we hear offstage voices singing)

CHORUS

Here he comes,
Mister Whiz.
Sound the drums,
Here he is.

Raconteur,
Bon vivant.
Tell us, sir,
What we want
To know:
The modus operandi
A dandy should use
When he is feeling low.

   (Behind him, a line of CHORUS BOYS *and* CHORUS GIRLS *appears.* BEN *joins the line, leading the number like a suave song-and-dance man)*

BEN

When the winds are blowing,

CHORUS

Yes?

BEN

That's the time to smile.

CHORUS

Oh?

BEN

Learn how to laugh,
Learn how to love,

Learn how to live,
That's my style.
When the rent is owing,

CHORUS

Yes?

BEN

What's the use of tears?

CHORUS

Oh?

BEN

I'd rather laugh,
I'd rather love,
I'd rather live
In arrears.

Some fellows sweat
To get to be millionaires,
Some have a sport
They're devotees of.
Some like to be the champs
At saving postage stamps,
Me, I like to live,
Me, I like to laugh,
Me, I like to love.

Some like to sink
And think in their easy chairs
Of all the things
They've risen above.
Some like to be profound
By reading Proust and Pound.
Me, I like to live,

Me, I like to laugh,
Me, I like to love.

Success is swell
And success is sweet,
But every height has a drop.
The less achievement,
The less defeat.
What's the point of shovin'
Your way to the top?
Live 'n' laugh 'n' love 'n'
You're never a flop.
So when the walls are crumbling,

CHORUS
Yes?

BEN
Don't give up the ship.

CHORUS
No.

BEN
Learn how to laugh,
Learn how to love,
Learn how to live,
That's my tip.
When I hear the rumbling,

CHORUS
Yes?

BEN
Do I lose my grip?

BEN and CHORUS
No!

BEN

I have to laugh,
I have to love,
I have to live.
That's my trip.

Some get a boot
From shooting off cablegrams
Or buzzing bells
To summon the staff.
Some climbers get their kicks
From social politics
Me, I like to love,
Me, I like to . . .
  (*He forgets his lyric, calls for it from the conductor,*
  recovers his poise)
Some break their asses
Passing their bar exams,
Lay out their lives
Like lines on a graph . . .
One day they're diplomats—
Well, bully and congrats!
Me, I like to love,
Me, I . . .

  (BEN *suddenly goes blank. He can't remember what*
  comes next. He tries to keep on dancing, stutters out a
  phrase or two, calls for help to the conductor, who
  shouts the lyrics to him.
  It's no good. His desperation grows. Behind him, as if
  nothing at all were wrong, the chorus line of boys and
  girls goes right on dancing. Making one final effort, BEN
  half-sings)
Me, I like—me, I love—me.

(With which he lunges forward out of the dance and shouts)
I don't love me!
(The chorus line goes on dancing, as if he didn't exist. He turns to the girl nearest him and shouts)
Her zipper stuck and you, you kept on saying how you loved her.
(To the next girl)
He was lying!
(And the next)
I just wanted her, that's all. I only wanted her until I had her. After that—
(Ranging up and down the line of CHORUS BOYS *and* CHORUS GIRLS, *hurling it at them)*
The job was there: I took it. I took it. I'm too clever. They don't catch me. They don't—
(From the corner of his eye, he catches sight of a fragment of the party, high up on a downstage platform. Shouting up at them)
You can't catch me. I'm too smart.
(The Follies drops begin to rise, and bit by bit we're back on the stage of the Weismann theater. Not literally, however. We're inside BEN's *mind, and through his eyes we see a kind of madness.*

Everything we've seen and heard all evening is going on at once, as if the night's experience were being vomited. Ghosts, memories and party guests—all there. They stand on platforms which are moving insanely back and forth, they mill about the stage, and all of them are doing bits and pieces of their scenes and songs. And through it all, downstage, BEN's *chorus line continues dancing.*

The cacophony is terrible, and we can barely hear BEN *as he races from one group of people to another screaming)*

They're rotten books, for God's sake. Don't you know it?
. . . It's a trick. It's nothing and I let her do it . . . She said
she'd kill herself. I didn't think she meant it . . . Jesus—
Ben! . . .
> *(There is a sudden beat of utter silence into which he
> cries out)*

Phyllis!
> *(He races off stage as the chaos resumes. It reaches a
> peak of madness and then, as the lights dim down, it
> starts receding. Softer, softer. Then, for a moment, the
> stage is dark and there is no sound. In the silence,
> softly, we hear* BEN *say)*

Phyllis . . .
> *(Dim light comes to a stage deserted except for* BEN, PHYL-
> LIS, BUDDY *and* SALLY, *all back in their evening clothes.*
> SALLY, *as if cut from stone, sits staring out at nothing. Far,
> far upstage, the back wall of the theater has gone and in
> the gray light of predawn, we see buildings across the
> street. In the darkness at the sides, a figure stirs. An-
> other. And in the shadows, we can make out* YOUNG BEN,
> YOUNG PHYLLIS, YOUNG BUDDY *and* YOUNG SALLY. *They
> stand watching)*

PHYLLIS I'm here, Ben; I'm right here.

BUDDY Sally? Are you all right? *(No response at all, not a
flicker. Crouching beside her)* Come on, kid. Hey, it's me.

SALLY *(Voice dead, eyes straight ahead)* I left the dishes in the
sink, I left them there, I was in such a hurry and there
is no Ben for me, not ever, any place.

BUDDY There never was, and that's the truth. Come on. I'll
take you home.

SALLY I can't stand up.

BUDDY I'll help you.

SALLY I should of died the first time.

BUDDY Cut that out.

SALLY I should of been dead all these years.

BUDDY Don't talk that way. You've got a lot to live for:
friends, a home, some money—Go on, say it after me, out
loud. You say it. Friends . . .

SALLY Friends . . .

BUDDY Home . . .

SALLY Home . . .

BUDDY We're gonna go and get some rest . . . And then
we're gonna make plans for tomorrow.

SALLY For tomorrow . . . *(She pauses, looks up at the morning light that seeps into the ruined theater. There is no hope
at all)* Oh dear God, it *is* tomorrow.

   (BUDDY *holds her tightly in his arms*)

BEN I've lost my jacket. (PHYLLIS *picks it up*) There has to
be a way . . . I won't face one more morning feeling—
(Impatiently) Despair: I'm sick to goddamn death of it.

PHYLLIS *(With a flash of white-hot anger)* Amen. It's easy; life
is empty, there is no hope. Hope doesn't grow on trees;
we make our own and I am here to tell you it's the hardest
thing we'll ever do.

BEN I've always been afraid of you. You see straight
through me and I've always thought, "It isn't possible; it
can't be me she loves."

PHYLLIS *(Still hot with the intensity of what she feels)* Well,
think again. Come on. We're going home.

BEN You're really something, aren't you?

PHYLLIS Bet your ass.

>(BUDDY *helps* SALLY *to her feet. She can barely stand, and he supports her as they turn and slowly start upstage. As they turn,* BEN *holds out his hand to* PHYLLIS. *She looks at him, then takes it.*
>
>*As the two couples move away from us toward the morning light, their young selves drift down silently, then turn. They all stand silhouetted, motionless. Then, soft and faint, as if it all were spoken years ago, we hear*)

YOUNG BUDDY *(Singing)*
Hey, up there!

YOUNG BEN
Way up there!

YOUNG BEN and YOUNG BUDDY
Whaddaya say, up there!

YOUNG SALLY
Hi . . .

YOUNG BEN
Girls . . .

YOUNG PHYLLIS
Ben . . .

YOUNG BUDDY
Sally . . .

Curtain

About the Authors

JAMES GOLDMAN studied to be a music critic until his postgraduate work at Columbia was interrupted by the draft. Two years later he left the service determined to write for stage and screen. Mr. Goldman won an Oscar for his screenplay of *The Lion in Winter*, which he adapted from his Broadway play. Before *The Lion in Winter* he was represented on Broadway twice, co-authoring with his brother, novelist William Goldman, the book and lyrics for *A Family Affair* and a comedy, *Blood, Sweat and Stanley Poole*. He wrote the screenplay for *They Might Be Giants*, based on his own play of that title, which was originally produced in London by Joan Littlewood. In addition, he is the author of a novel, *Waldorf*. James Goldman has previously collaborated with Stephen Sondheim on a musical adaptation for television of John Collier's short story "Evening Primrose." He has more recently written the screenplay for Sam Spiegel's production of *Nicholas and Alexandra*. Mr. Goldman lives in New York City with his wife and two children.

STEPHEN SONDHEIM won the 1971 Tony awards for Best Music and Best Lyrics for *Company*—winner of the Drama Critics' Circle and Tony awards for Best Musical. Born in 1930 in New York City, he attended Williams College, where he won the Hutchinson Prize for Musical Composition. After graduating, he studied theory and composition with Milton Babbitt. Mr. Sondheim is the creator of the memorable lyrics for *West Side Story*. He was the lyricist for *Gypsy* and *Do I Hear a Waltz?* and was responsible for both the lyrics and music of *A Funny Thing Happened on the Way to the Forum* and *Anyone Can Whistle*. His credits also include the incidental music for Broadway's *Girls of Summer* and *Invitation to a March*. In addition, he wrote scripts for the television series *Topper*.